SALVATION

WORD STUDIES FROM THE GREEK NEW TESTAMENT

GERALD COWEN

Foreword by Paige Patterson

BROADMAN PRESS
NASHVILLE, TENNESSEE

© Copyright 1990 ● Broadman Press
All rights reserved
4210-35
ISBN: 0-8054-1035-X
Dewey Decimal Classification: 234
Subject Heading: SALVATION
Library of Congress Catalog Card Number: 89-48592
Printed in the United States of America

Library of Congress Cataloging-in-Publication Data
Cowen, Gerald, 1942-
   Salvation : word studies from the Greek New Testament / Gerald Cowen.
      p.   cm.
      ISBN 0-8054-1035-X
      1. Salvation—Biblical teaching. 2. Bible. N.T.—Theology.
   I. Title.
   BS2545.S25C69 1990
   234—dc20   89-48592
                                                                                    CIP

Dedicated to . . .
Mr. and Mrs. J. P. Cowen, my Mom and Dad
who molded my life and encouraged me
in the ministry of the Lord Jesus Christ

Foreword

In 1985 Dr. Gerald Cowen followed a rich tradition pioneered by Richard C. Trench, Kenneth Wuest, W. E. Vine, and others and produced *Sermon Starters from the Greek New Testament*. That volume brought together the best in contemporary philosophical research and a practiced sense of what constitutes grist for the preacher's mill. The gratifying results are attested in the popularity of that volume.

Consequently, students and preachers alike will doubtless greet the appearance of *Salvation: Word Studies from the Greek New Testament* with "homiletical" enthusiasm. Once again, extensive lexical and syntactical research accomplished in part in the Bodleian Library in Oxford while Dr. Cowen was on sabbatical is discernible to the well-tutored eye. Cowen knows that words attract significance from the clauses, sentences, and paragraphs in which they occur just as they inform those same units with initial significance derived from the whole history of the word. He sensitively captures the nuances of particular usage as the words appear in the Greek New Testament.

For readers from the evangelical tradition the present monograph is especially germane. Few, if any, previous word studies have been focused on a particular topic. No topic is any more important for the evangelical Christian than the divine rescue operation planned in the councils of heaven, purchased in the ignominious mine shafts of human failure, and perpetuated in a time and place so glorious that all words, even biblical words, prove to be vehicles totally inadequate to carry the cargo. We call this spiritual galaxy of ideas "salvation." Cowen's work thus constitutes something of a brief introduction to soteriology via investigation of the varied terminology employed by the New Testament authors as they attempted under the guidance of the Holy Spirit to capture and to describe the magnificent concepts that belong to our salvation.

Word studies on "propitiation," "faith and works," and "adopted" are particularly perceptive. Distinguishing this effort from other word studies is the examination of brief phrases such as "wash away your sins" and "partakers of the Holy Spirit." This treatise is valuable as an occasional source on a particular word but also has the capacity to be used as a study guide for a doctrinal study on salvation. And Cowen interacts with the contemporary trends toward universalism and annihilationism, clearly demonstrating that neither is an option for a faithful biblical exegete.

This book will "preach," but more importantly Cowen has provided the research and insights that will make the preaching of these concepts both enlightening and challenging. Once again the brilliant hues of God's rainbow promise of salvation are made to appear against the backdrop of the dark cloud of human rebellion and hopelessness. May God bless this book to your soul and to your pulpit.

Paige Patterson
The Criswell College
Dallas, Texas

Preface

The purpose of this volume is to deal with one of the most basic of all Bible themes, the subject of salvation. The goal is to define biblical terms such as salvation or repentance with an emphasis on the practical applications of that knowledge. These are terms people commonly use, but often are unable to give an accurate description of the meaning. The book is intended for the pastor or layperson who wishes to know God's Word more fully by searching out even minute distinctions between words that are the building blocks of our theology. It is especially important that one clearly understands these words that bear upon the subject of salvation. Not only do they have bearing on the exact meaning of individual texts, but more importantly on the salvation of lost souls.

It is also important for the English reader to realize that the English text may mask distinctions that are clearly made on the Greek text. This is true for two reasons. First, the Greek language may have several words (all with different shades of meaning) for a concept for which English has only one, and this can be misleading. In addition, the intention of the author may be clearly implied by the grammar used, but the exact meaning is not conveyed by a literal or word-for-word translation, because the same intent is not conveyed in English. It must be explained to the reader.

The approach has generally been to survey the use of a word in secular and Jewish sources, such as the Septuagint translation of the Old Testament, to see if any light can be shed on the meaning of the word in the New Testament. An effort has been made to organize the material, when possible, so that it may be used by the reader for devotional purposes.

The English translation generally used is the *King James Version*. In some cases the author's revision of that translation is used. When other translations are used, they are cited.

Gerald Cowen
The Criswell College
Dallas, Texas

Contents

Introduction:
What Is Salvation?

One of the most common expressions in the New Testament to describe the state of the believer in Jesus Christ is the word *saved*. In fact, the verb form alone (*sozo*) occurs over ninety times in the New Testament and the noun form forty-six times (*soterio*). Just what does it mean to be saved?

Let us begin by looking at the background of this word. In classical Greek *sozo* means to escape destruction (to keep a whole skin), to be healed (recover from sickness), keep safe or preserve (such as a city), to be preserved or extant (such as a book), to bring one home safe from a journey, and carry off safe (rescue from something such as death).

In secular Greek papyri from the New Testament period *sozo* had a variety of uses, just as does the English word *save*. (1) It means to recover from sickness. A document from 132 B.C. says, "Your life has been saved in sickness by the great god Socnopaeus." (2) It is used of rescue from danger. Another papyrus says, "Thanks to

Serapis, when I was in danger at sea, he saved me." (3) It may refer to the saving of a person's life. It is said that "in the first place Caesar saved Cleopatra's life when he conquered the kingdom." (4) The use of preserving something from going out of existence is illustrated by a reference to "certain books saved at the temple." (5) *Sozo* can also have the meaning "reserving" or "keeping something back" for a special purpose as in the case of "sacred revenues" that are "to be preserved for the gods as in former times." (6) Finally, this term can refer to the state of being that results from "being saved" (safe and sound). A reference has been found that refers to "sixty pigeons safe and sound," and another, "I will hand over the freight safe and unharmed."

The use of *soteria* (salvation) in the Old Testament has been summarized in the following manner.[1] (1) In the Greek Old Testament, *soteria* means "general safety and security." Proverbs 11:14 says that in the multitude of counselors there is safety *(soteria)*. (2) It speaks of "deliverance from trouble in general." The man who waits on God will rejoice in his deliverance (Isa. 25:9; Ps. 20:6; Jer. 25:35). (3) Often, *soteria* refers to "deliverance from an enemy." It describes God's deliverance of Israel from her enemies (see Judg. 15:18; 1 Sam. 11:9,13; 2 Kings 13:5). (4) In particular, "salvation" describes Israel's deliverance at the Red Sea. Moses said, "Stand still and see the salvation of the Lord" (Ex. 14:13). (5) The full extent of salvation is spoken of as future. The glory of God will be completely revealed only in the age to come (Isa. 45:17; 52:10; Jer. 3:23). (6) The source of salvation is God. He is described as the God of salvation (Ps. 18:46; 38:22; 51:14). (7) Finally, salvation is a prominent theme in the songs of thanksgiving found in the Old Testament. Hannah thanked God for His salvation when she learned she was to have a son (1 Sam. 2:1; see also Ex. 15:2; 2 Sam. 22:3,36,47,51).

With all the varied uses of *sozo* and *soteria* in the Old Testament and secular literature, these terms have a rich background for use in the New Testament. Some of the old uses are repeated in the New Testament, such as deliverance from the sea (Acts 27:34), deliverance from prison (Phil. 1:19), and safety (Heb. 11:7). However, the vast majority of uses of "salvation" and "save" in the New Testament are in connection with that spiritual deliverance granted by God through faith in His Son, the Lord Jesus Christ. First of all, the New Testament is clear that salvation is one of the main items in the purpose of God. Jesus said, "For the Son of man is come to seek and to save that which was lost" (Luke 19:10). Again, He said, "For God sent not his Son into the world to condemn the world; but that the world through him might be saved" (John 3:17). Paul added that Jesus came into the world "to save sinners" (1 Tim. 1:15). The purpose of Jesus' coming to earth is to make the salvation of humankind possible.

In the second place, Jesus is the essential part of God's plan of salvation. It is through Him alone that a person may be saved. Acts 4:12 states, "Neither is there salvation in any other: for there is none other name under heaven given among men, whereby we must be saved." This is reminiscent of Jesus' own teaching in John 10:1-9. He said that anyone who tries to enter the sheepfold by any other way than the door is a "thief and a robber"; then He said, "I am the door." Jesus is so much at the center of salvation that sometimes He is equated with it. For example, Luke records Jesus' visit to the house of Zacchaeus (19:1-10). At the end of the visit Jesus said, "This day is salvation come to this house." (See also John 4:22.)

Another thing that ought to be noticed about salvation

is that human agency is necessary in bringing it about. Obviously, God could effect it without human effort, but it is also obvious that He has chosen not to do it that way. Paul, speaking of his ministry to Israel, said, "I magnify mine office: If by any means I may provoke to emulation them which are my flesh, and might *save* some of them" (Rom. 11:13-14, author's italics). He told the Corinthians that believing husbands and wives should not leave their marriage partners because by staying they might be able to "save" them (1 Cor. 7:16). He became "all things to all men" that he might "save some" (1 Cor. 9:22; see also 10:33). The Jews, on the other hand, hindered him from speaking to the Gentiles "that they might be saved" (1 Thess. 2:16). Paul warned Timothy to be careful about his doctrine because in doing so he would save himself and "them that hear" (1 Tim. 4:16). James said that the man who converts a sinner from the error of his way "shall save a soul from death, and hide a multitude of sins" (5:20). Finally, Jude encouraged the soul-winner to use whatever approach is necessary to persuade the sinner to be saved when he said, "And of some have compassion, making a difference: And others save with fear, pulling them out of the fire" (vv. 22-23). These references are sufficient to show that God uses people to bring about His goal of saving others.

If people are instrumental in bringing salvation to other people, it follows that this gift of salvation may be refused by those to whom it is offered. The author of Hebrews emphasized this point when he said, "How shall we escape, if we neglect so great salvation?" (2:3). Again he said, "And being made perfect, he became the author of eternal salvation unto all them that obey him" (5:9).

Now let us discuss these factors mentioned in the New Testament that bring about salvation. First, there is the preaching of the cross. The message of Christ's death on the cross is essential. "Unto us which are saved, it is the power of God," Paul said (1 Cor. 1:18). He went on to explain this further, "It pleased God by the foolishness of the thing preached to save them that believe" (v. 1:21).

Next, there is the essential element of the grace of God. The familiar text of Ephesians 2:8 underlines this truth: "For by grace are you saved through faith; and that not of yourselves: it is the gift of God." Add to that the word of Peter at the Jerusalem conference on the salvation of the Gentiles (Acts 15:11), "But we believe that through the grace of the Lord Jesus Christ we shall be saved, even as they," and one must realize that salvation comes only as a gift from God. Any work on the part of a person seeking salvation is of no consequence in bringing about his or her salvation.

A third factor that leads to salvation is repentance (a change of mind). Paul wrote, "For godly sorrow works repentance to salvation not to be repented of: but the sorrow of the world works death" (2 Cor. 7:10). A person must change his or her mind about God and about sin. Closely connected with repentance is faith. Ephesians 2:8 says, "For by grace are you saved through faith." Paul said the gospel is "the power of God unto salvation to everyone who believes" (Rom. 1:16). To Timothy he wrote concerning the "holy scriptures, which are able to make thee wise unto salvation through faith which is in Christ Jesus" (2 Tim. 3:15). In addition, Peter spoke of the connection faith has with salvation: "Receiving the end of your faith, even the salvation of your souls" (1 Pet. 1:9).

A fifth factor mentioned in the New Testament regarding salvation is endurance. Jesus said to the disciples, "And ye shall be hated of all men for my name's sake, but he that endures to the end shall be saved" (Matt. 10:22;

see also 24:13). The man who believes truly in Jesus Christ will not be defeated "by his own doubts nor by the arguments and seductions of others. His trust is something to which he must cling as to a life belt in an overwhelming sea"[1] And he will.

One of the reasons for the believer's endurance is another factor that brings about salvation, the intercession of Christ. The author of Hebrews said, "Wherefore he is able also to save them to the uttermost that come unto God by him, seeing he ever liveth to make intercession for them" (Heb. 7:25). John 17 is an example of this intercessory prayer that undergirds the believer.

Now that some of the facts about salvation and factors involved in salvation have been surveyed, another question needs to be asked. From what is a person saved? In the spiritual sense, there are three categories of deliverance from sin. First, there are those that relate to salvation from the penalty of sin. Jesus came to save sinners from being "lost" (Matt. 18:11). James added that to convert a sinner is to "save a soul from death" (Jas. 5:20). Not only is the believer saved from being lost and from death, but also the believer is saved from the wrath of God. Paul said, "Much more then, being now justified by his blood, we shall be saved from wrath through him" (Rom. 5:9).

Next, there is salvation from the power and oppression of sin in this world. Luke recorded the words of Peter to the Jews at Pentecost; he exhorted them to "save yourselves from this untoward [perverse] generation" (Acts 2:40). Paul testified, even though he was facing death, of God's faithfulness, "And the Lord shall deliver me from every evil work, and will preserve [*sozo*] me unto his heavenly kingdom" (2 Tim. 4:18). This idea is also found in many other passages, such as Romans 6:14, although the word *salvation* is not used there.

Finally, in the future the believer shall be saved from the
presence of sin and its contamination. In Matthew 19:23-
25, entering the kingdom of heaven is equated with being
saved; Jesus told the disciples that a "rich man shall hardly
enter into the kingdom of heaven." In fact, it is easier for a
"camel to go through the eye of a needle." Their reply
was, "Who then can be saved?" The final installment of
our salvation involves entering the place where there is
nothing that "works abomination or a lie" (Rev. 21:27).

So then, salvation can be spoken of as past, present, and
future. It is past for the person who has already received
Christ. That person has been saved. Paul used this terminology in Titus 3:5, where he said, "Not by works of righteousness which we have done, but according to his mercy
he saved us." Again, in 2 Timothy 1:9, speaking of God,
he said, "Who hath saved us, and called us with an holy
calling." In the Greek text also, Romans 8:24 reads, "For
we are saved by hope." Salvation is described as a continuous action in present time in 1 Corinthians 1:18. Paul said
that to the "ones who are being saved" (author's interpretation) the preaching of the cross is the "power of God."
The believer is in the process of being saved. (See 1 Cor.
15:2 also.) This process will be completed at the end of
the age, when Christ comes to claim His bride, the church.
Even those without proper works will still "be saved; yet
so as by fire" (1 Cor. 3:15). The church is to discipline
those who are living in sin "that the spirit may be saved in
the day of the Lord Jesus" (1 Cor. 5:5). Peter said that we
have a salvation that is "ready to be revealed in the last
time" (1 Pet. 1:5). And finally, it is in the end times that a
voice from heaven will say, "Now is come salvation, and
strength, and the kingdom of our God, and the power of
his Christ: for the accuser of our brethren is cast down"
(Rev. 12:10).

Chapter 1
The Need for Salvation

Lost

Jesus stated the purpose of His coming to this world in Luke 19:10: "For the Son of man is come to seek and to save that which was lost." The question for this inquiry is, What does it mean to be "lost"? The Greek word used to describe this condition is *apollumi* (sometimes *apolluo*), which is a stronger form of *ollumi,* and means to utterly destroy. In Homer's writings it is used to describe death in battle. Similarly, other classical writers use it to mean to demolish, or lay waste. Additional uses include to waste one's substance, to talk or bore someone to death, to ruin a woman, or to lose one's life (Liddell and Scott). Some argue that the primary meaning is to cease to exist. However, that is only one meaning. It can mean to be undone or simply to be lost, such as water that is poured out on the ground.

In the secular papyruses of New Testament times *apollumi* commonly speaks of the loss of money. One document speaks of the loss of two pigs because of the difficulty of a journey. Other documents use this term in reference to the loss of money or goods due to robbery (Moulton & Milligan).

The word *lost* (*apollumi*) has several shades of meaning in the New Testament. First, it means to be "ruined or rendered useless." This is illustrated by the old wineskins that cannot be used for new wine again lest they break and therefore perish (Matt. 9:17). In the second place, "lost" may refer to things "wasted or allowed to spoil," such as food. After the feeding of the five thousand Jesus was careful that the "fragments" be collected "that nothing be lost" (John 6:12). Next, *apollumi* may refer to items that may be lost, either physical or spiritual. Jesus promised the disciples that not one "hair of your head" shall perish (Luke 21:18). But, it is better for an eye or a hand to perish than for the whole person to go to hell (Matt. 5:29). It is also used in warnings to believers to be careful lest they lose the things they have worked for, instead of receiving a full reward (2 John 8; Matt. 10:42).

The word *apollumi* is sometimes used with the meaning "kill" or "destroy." Matthew 10:28 says, "Fear not them which kill the body, but are not able to kill the soul: but rather fear him which is able to destroy both soul and body in hell." One should remember that the New Testament does not refer to cessation of existence when it speaks of eternal death. Rather than death, which lasts forever, it refers to dying eternally. There is quite a difference. It is an eternal punishment, not one that lasts only for a moment and then is over forever (Matt. 25:46).

Not only do people who are lost bring loss upon themselves, but it should be noted that one of the chief results is that they are lost to another, namely God. The sheep that wanders away brings loss to the shepherd. He leaves "the ninety and nine" and goes after the one that is lost (Luke 15:4). Jesus came to seek and to save the lost (19:10), and He commanded the disciples to go to the "lost sheep of the house of Israel" (Matt. 10:6). Of the twelve disciples, Jesus said, "Those that you gave me I have kept, and none of them is lost, but the son of perdition" (John 17:12). God does not want to "lose" any of His creation.

Finally, the word *lost* is applied to those who "fail to be saved." Peter said, "[God is] not willing that any should perish, but that all should come to repentance" (2 Pet. 3:9). It is also translated "perish" in John 3:16, where to "perish" is the opposite of obtaining eternal life. In 1 Corinthians 1:18 "to perish" is contrasted with being "saved." Paul gave a solemn warning to believers to make sure the gospel was not obscured by ungodly living, because "if our gospel be hid, it is hid to them that are lost" (2 Cor. 4:3). Let us make sure that we are never guilty of causing anyone to fail to be saved, because it is a terrible thing to be lost.

Condemned

Romans 8:1 says, "There is therefore now no condemnation to them which are in Christ Jesus." In contrast to this magnificent declaration is John 3:18, which says, "He that believeth on him is not condemned: but he that believeth not is condemned already, because he hath not believed in the name of the only begotten Son of God." Condemnation as a result of sin is a clear teaching of the Word of God. In the New Testament alone there are several words that express this idea, each with a different shade of meaning.

Katakrima

The word for condemnation in Romans 8:1 is *katakrima* (the verb form is *katakrino*). Deissmann defines the word as "a burden ensuing from a judicial pronouncement—a burden." Moulton and Milligan agree that the word does not mean condemnation as such, but the "punishment following the sentence," or "penal servitude." An example from the papyruses uses the word *katakrima* as a " 'judgment' for a sum of money to be paid as a fine or damages." The verb form of the word means "to give judgment against someone" or "judge worthy of punishment, to condemn." It is used of the condemnation of Sodom and Gomorrah (2 Pet. 2:6), the one who judges another (Rom. 2:1), and the one who eats meat even though his conscience tells him to refrain (Rom. 14:23). It implies the fact of a crime, whether real, as in the cases mentioned, or fabricated, as in the case of the condemnation of Christ by the Jews (Matt. 20:18). Symbolically, *katakrima* also is used of condemnation resulting from a good example. Noah, for instance, condemned the world of his day by the building of the ark (Heb. 11:7).

Kataginosko

A second word that expresses the idea of being condemned is *kataginosko,* which literally means "to know something against" someone. In classical Greek it generally means "to form an unfavorable judgment or opinion against someone." However, it was sometimes used in a legal context to signify laying "a charge against a person" or "to pronounce a verdict" or sentence upon a person for a crime such as murder. This word carries the implication that the wrong is evident for all to see. This is the term that is used to describe Peter's sin in Galatians 2:11. Here Paul said, "I withstood him to the face, because he was to be blamed." He stood condemned as a result of his actions, which were observed by all present. His own conscience, which had been enlightened prior to this time, also confirmed the verdict in his own heart. This use of the word also occurs in 1 John 3:20-21.

Katadikazo

Another term that donates condemnation is *katadikazo*. This is a legal term that means to "exercise right or law against anyone; hence to pronounce judgment, to condemn" (Vine). It is a combination of *kata* (down or against) and *dike* (justice). In secular Greek documents it is illustrated by its occurrence in a letter discussing the release of a man who had been condemned to work in the alabaster quarries. In the New Testament it occurs only four times (Matt. 12:7,37; Luke 6:37; Jas. 5:6). When people stand before God, they will be either acquitted or condemned by their own words; thereby justice will be brought down on them (Matt. 12:37).

Krino

The most common word meaning "to condemn" in the New Testament is *krino*. Its primary meaning is "to judge in the sense of discerning something" or "to reach a decision about something." The decision in the case of *krino* can be either for or against someone, whereas *katakrino* is always condemnation. However, many times *krino* denotes a decision of condemnation in which the guilty party is handed over for punishment. It is used in this sense in Acts 13:27. Here Paul said that the Jewish leaders fulfilled the words of the Old Testament prophets in condemning Jesus. James warned, "Grudge not one against another, brethren, lest ye be condemned: behold, the judge standeth before the door" (Jas. 5:9). The noun form (*krisis*) occurs in this sense in John 5:24, which says, "He that hears my word, and believes on him that sent me, has everlasting life, and shall not come into condemnation; but is passed from death unto life."

The condemnation that has come upon all humanity is the result of sin (Rom. 5:16,18). The sentence (*katakrima*) has already been passed. The only way it can be lifted is through the forgiveness that comes by faith in Christ (John 3:18). To the one who is in Him there is *now* no condemnation (Rom. 8:1).

Hell

There are three Greek words that are all translated in the *King James Version* by the English word *hell*.

Geenna

The first of these is *geenna*, which is the final abode of the wicked dead. The word has no roots in Greek thought because it is Jewish in origin. It represents the Hebrew *Ge-Hinnom* (the valley of Tophet, the "place of burning"), which means the valley of lamentation. The Valley of Hinnom is located on the south and east of Jerusalem. It obtained its name from the cries of the little children who were offered as human sacrifices by being thrown into the fiery arms of the idol Moloch. Ahaz, king of Judah, was guilty of sacrificing his own children to Moloch: "Moreover he burnt incense in the valley of the son of Hinnom, and burnt his children in the fire, after the abominations of the heathen whom the Lord had cast out before the children of Israel" (2 Chron. 28:3). King Josiah attempted to abolish these horrible practices and to ensure that the place never be used for such again. The place was defiled by making it into a garbage dump (2 Kings 23:10). Evidently, the bodies of dead animals and executed criminals were left there also. To avoid the smell, the place was constantly being burned, and thus it was called the "gehenna of fire." After the death of Josiah, the practice of making children pass through the fire was revived (see Jer. 7:31).

In the New Testament the term is used twelve times. All of these references except one (Jas. 3:6) are found in the Synoptic Gospels and are used by Jesus Himself. Six of these references refer to *Geenna* as a place of fire. Mark 9:43-48 adds that it is a place of unquenchable fire: "Where their worm dieth not, and the fire is not quenched." It is a place of damnation and judgment (Matt. 23:33), from which it is impossible to escape. Finally, it is God who has the "power to cast into hell" (Luke 12:5) "both soul and body" (Matt. 10:28).

Geenna probably should be equated with the "lake of fire" that is mentioned in Revelation 20:14-15. Into this place both death and hades are cast. It is the place that was prepared for "the devil and his angels" (Matt. 25:41), but has also become the final abode of the unrighteous: "And these shall go away into everlasting punishment: but the righteous into life eternal" (Matt. 25:46).

Hades

A second word that has been translated by the English word *hell* is *hades* (sometimes *haides*). In the Greek classics the word refers to: (1) Pluto, the god of the underworld;

(2) the dismal place that is the realm of the dead; or (3) finally, after the time of Homer, to death or the grave (see Liddell and Scott). The origin of the word is still a subject of debate. Some argue that it comes from *a* (not) plus *idein* (to see) and, therefore, it means "the unseen." Others agree with Vine, who says, "A more probable deviation is from *hado,* signifying all-receiving."

In the Greek version of the Old Testament, the Hebrew word *sheol* is almost always translated by *hades* (see Job 10:21; 11:8; and Isa. 57:9). In the Old Testament *sheol* (*hades*) is a neutral word and refers to the place of all the dead. It does not refer to a place of annihilation or even a place of sleep, but rather a place of real, though shadowy, existence. "It is real life with little substance"[1] (*Criswell Study Bible,* note on Matt. 11:23). The fact that *hades* is used so much in the Greek Old Testament lays the foundation for its use and meaning in the New Testament.

Hades occurs four times in the Gospels, twice in Acts, and four times in Revelation. Jesus used it to describe the ultimate end of the city of Capernaum (Matt. 11:23; Luke 10:15); He told Peter that "the gates of [*hades*] shall not prevail" against the church (Matt. 16:18); and He said that *hades* was the place the rich man went when he died. It is in His teachings a place of terrible punishment. Luke said that the soul of Christ was not left there (Acts 1:27,31). John said that Jesus has the keys of *hades* (Rev. 1:18).

In Revelation 6:8 *hades* is personified as the rider of one of the four horses. The final occurrence of the word *hades* is in Revelation 20:13-14. Here *hades* itself is cast into the lake of fire. Several conclusions can be drawn about *hades* from these statements: (1) It originally referred to the place where all the dead go. Jesus Himself went there, but there is no indication that He suffered there. On the contrary, He went to a place of paradise (Luke 23:43). (2) *Ha-*

des became known as a place of awful punishment. (3) *Hades* is not a permanent place (Rev. 20:13-14).

W. E. Vine says about *hades*, "It never denotes the grave, nor is it the permanent region of the lost; in point of time it is, for such, intermediate between decease and the doom of Gehenna." It is quite possible that *hades* was the abode of the righteous dead also, until the time of the ascension of Christ, at which time He took them with Him to their permanent abode.

Tartaroo

The third and least-known word referring to the punishment of hell is *Tartaroo* (cast down to hell). It is the verb form of *Tartarus,* denoting the place, and it is found only once in the New Testament (2 Pet. 2:4). The Greek poet Homer described *Tartarus* as "far below, where the uttermost depth of the pit lies under earth, where there are gates of iron and a brazen doorstone, as far beneath the house of Hades as from earth the sky lies" (*Iliad* 8.13-16). It was originally the place of punishment of the Titans, the early gods of the Greeks, who according to Greek literature were overthrown and replaced by the Olympian gods.

According to Arndt, *Tartarus* refers to a place lower than *hades* in Greek thought, in the Greek Old Testament, and in the writings of Philo and Josephus (see Job 41:24). Thayer agrees that *Tartarus* corresponds to the *gehenna* of the Jews. This writer, however, must side with W. E. Vine who declares that *Tartarus* is "neither Sheol nor Hades nor hell, but the place where those angels whose special sin is to be referred to in that passage are confined 'to be reserved unto judgment.' "

The key word here is "reserved," indicating that *Tarta-*

rus is the temporary abode of at least most of these fallen angels rather than the final one, just as *hades* is the temporary abode for the wicked dead (Rev. 20:13). The final abode for both the wicked and the fallen angels is the same, *gehenna* (Matt. 25:41).

The Wrath of God

Perhaps the most important factor that underscores the need for salvation is the wrath of God against sin. As the writer of Hebrews put it, "How shall we escape, if we neglect so great salvation?" (Heb. 2:3) There are two words that are used to describe the wrath of God in the New Testament.

Thumos

The first is *thumos,* which occurs eighteen times. In classical Greek *thumos* represented a "feeling" or "thought," especially strong feeling or passion. In a physical sense it represented the life or strength of a person. More importantly, it denoted the "desire" or "inclination" of a person. It is used to refer to physical appetites, such as desire for food, or a desire that one wishes for "with all one's heart." It could variously refer to the mind, temper, will, spirit, or courage of a person, as well as represent the seat of anger or wrath. It is this last use that is most prominent in the New Testament.

Eight times *thumos* is used to refer to the wrath of God. All except one are in the Revelation. John spoke of the "wine of the wrath of God," which will be poured out (Rev. 14:10), the "great winepress of the wrath of God" (v. 19), and the vials full of the "wrath of God" (15:1,7;

16:1). Twice *thumos* is coupled with *orge* to describe the "fierceness" of God's wrath (16:19; 19:15). The other occurrence is in Romans 2:8 where it is used in a list of words, all of which describe the judgment of God upon evil.

Orge

The other word for wrath in the New Testament is *orge.* The classical meaning of *orge* originally was a "natural impulse or propensity." From that was derived the meaning "temperament, disposition, or mood." Since anger is the strongest of the passions, it finally came to refer to "anger, wrath, or passion." In the New Testament it occurs thirty-six times. In twenty-six of the thirty-six occurrences it refers to the anger, wrath, vengeance, or indignation of God. While some argue that there is no noticeable difference in the meaning of *orge* as compared with *thumos,* many classical and Koine Greek writers point out the difference between these words (see Trench for a survey of these opinions). *Thumos* is represented as the "more passionate, and at the same time more temporary" in character (Trench). It is a great, but temporary anger. *Orge,* on the other hand, represents "more of an abiding and settled habit of mind." James Denney describes the difference in this way, "Orge is wrath within; *thumos* as it overflows."[1]

Most of the references to God's wrath employ *orge.* Jesus looked on the Jews with anger because they sought to oppose His healing of the man with the withered hand (Mark 3:5). The "wrath of God abideth" on the one who refuses to believe in Jesus (John 3:36). In the wilderness, God swore in His wrath that Israel should not enter into His rest (Heb. 3:11; 4:3). Paul said that Jesus delivered us from the wrath that is to come (1 Thess. 1:10). Other examples are Romans 1:18; 2:5,8; 5:9; 9:22; Ephesians 5:6; Colossians 3:6; and Revelation 6:16-17; 11:18.

God's wrath (*orge*) represents the settled and abiding indignation of God against sin, which is only held back by His long-suffering and desire to see men repent. This indignation will finally overflow like a volcano (*thumos*) to judge sin finally and convincingly at the end of the age. If God has shown His wrath in the past in the form of judgment upon evildoers, who is to say that He cannot or will not—because of His loving nature—behave in this same way toward us? Everything in Scripture underlines the seriousness of God's wrath (Rev. 6:16-17). History, present experience, and prophecy clearly testify to the wrath of God. They testify clearly that the wrath of God is poured out on those who have chosen to rebel against God, and especially on those who have refused to receive His Beloved Son (John 3:36). The great promise of the Word of God is that we may escape the wrath that is to come through Jesus Christ. Paul said, "Being now justified by his blood, we shall be saved from wrath through him" (Rom. 5:9).

Chapter 2
The Purpose of Salvation

The Power of God Unto Salvation

There are two primary words in the Greek language that denote "power."

Dunamis

The first of these is *dunamis,* which occurs 120 times in the New Testament. This is the word that is found in Romans 1:16, where it describes the gospel. Paul said, "For I am not ashamed of the gospel of Christ: for it is the power of God unto salvation to every one that believes." In the *King James Version, dunamis* is translated in a variety of ways ("power," "mighty work," "strength," "miracle," "might," "virtue," "mighty"); however, over half of the time it is translated by the word *power.*

The primary idea expressed by *dunamis* is the "power or ability to do something." It refers to inherent power as opposed to power received from another source. It represents "power residing in a thing by virtue of its nature" (Thayer). In classical Greek it refers to bodily strength, the power of influence, any natural capacity or faculty, the force of the elements of nature, and the power of medicine, words, or money. Ramsay has shown that in pagan religions power was one of the most common terms in pagan devotion. Power "was what the devotees respected and worshipped."[1] Any show of power was evidence of the divine.

In the New Testament *dunamis* refers, first of all, to the ability and inherent might of God Himself. Romans 1:20 speaks of His "eternal power and Godhead." Matthew 26:64 implies that He *is* power: "Hereafter shall you see the Son of Man sitting on the right hand of power." Jesus was approved by miracles (works of power, Acts 2:22). It was by His power that the lame man was healed (Acts 4:7,10). The Holy Spirit is also a source of that same power: "You shall receive power after the Holy Ghost is come upon you" (Acts 1:8).

In the second place *dunamis* may refer to that which manifests God's power, such as a mighty work. Philip, for example, performed "miracles (*dunamis*) and signs." Paul said that the gospel also demonstrates the power of God in that it is able to save people from their sins (Rom. 1:16). The preaching of Christ crucified is both the "power of God, and the wisdom of God" (1 Cor. 1:23-24). The use of the word *dunamis* in this context underlines the fact that God is able to save people and that the gospel is the means through which God intends to do so. The only qualification mentioned is faith. It is effective "to everyone who believes."

Finally, people may exercise this power or ability as God delegates it to them. It is not inherent in them. Peter denied that the lame man was healed through his own power (Acts 3:12). Remember again Jesus' promise of Acts 1:8, "You shall receive power after the Holy Spirit is come upon you" (1:8). Stephen was the kind of man who was filled with the power of God (6:8), which seems to be synonymous here with being filled with the Spirit. To some, God gives a special gift for exercising His power. First Corinthians 12:28 says, "God hath set some in the church . . . after that miracles." The Greek word used here is the plural of *dunamis*, "powers." The power of the Holy Spirit that resides in the believer is made available to him or her. However, it may be used only under the direction of the Spirit, because the power is inherent in the Spirit, not the person exercising it.

Exousia

In addition to *dunamis*, there is another word whose primary meaning is power: *exousia*. Sixty-nine times it is translated "power" and twenty-nine times "authority." It is also translated "right," "liberty," "jurisdiction," and "strength." The primary idea in the word is "permission or liberty to act." It involves the use of authority that is usually delegated, but sometimes arbitrarily usurped.

Classical Greek usage shows *exousia* to represent "authority to do something" or "control over something or someone," such as wealth or a political office. The word is common in the secular papyruses in "wills, contracts, and other legal documents, to denote the 'claim,' or 'right,' or 'control,' one has over anything" (Moulton and Milligan).

When it is used of God, it is in its unrestricted, absolute sense. After Jesus' cleansing of the temple, the Jews wanted to know "By what authority" He did these things and who gave Him this authority? (Matt. 21:23). Jesus refused to answer at that time, but later He made a clear declaration of His authority. In Matthew 28:18 He said, "All power [authority] is given unto me in heaven and in earth." There is no limit to His authority (see John 17:2 also).

To certain people God delegates authority. For example, Paul spoke of not wanting to abuse his "power in the gospel" (1 Cor. 9:18). This authority was given to him by the Lord for the edification of the church (2 Cor. 10:8). Government officials are spoken of as "authorities," and they are ordained by God to be such (Rom. 13:1-3). To those who receive Him (Jesus), God gives the right or authority to become sons of God (John 1:12). Those who keep His commandments will be blessed with the "right to the tree of life, and may enter in through the gates into the city" (Rev. 22:14). Salvation is further described as being removed from under the "power [authority] of Satan unto God" (Acts 26:18).

Not only is Satan's authority, which is a delegated one, mentioned, but other spiritual beings are called "powers" (Eph. 3:10; 1 Pet. 3:22). In addition, demonic forces are called "powers" (Eph. 6:12; Col. 2:15).

In conclusion, regarding salvation it may be said that the gospel of Jesus Christ provides the enabling power to provide salvation for all who believe. And, to all who believe God gives the right to become part of His family. In Christ, we have both the ability (*dunamis*) and the authority (*exousia*) necessary to receive salvation.

For Our Sins

The apostle Paul made an amazing statement at the conclusion of 2 Corinthians 5. He said, "For he has made him to be sin for us, who knew no sin; that we might be made the righteousness of God in him" (v. 21). The key word in understanding the significance of this statement is the preposition "for," which is the translation of the Greek word *huper* (or *hyper*). What makes the interpretation difficult is the fact that prepositions are the most complicated words in the Greek language. They have a variety of meanings, depending upon their usage and context. For example, with the accusative case *huper* means "above" or "beyond." In Philippians 2:9 the name of Jesus is "above" or "beyond" (superior) any other name. (See 1 Cor. 4:6 also.) However, with the accusative it occurs only 19 times in the New Testament, while it occurs 126 times with the genitive case.

With the genitive case *huper* originally meant "over" or "above," but this use is not found in the New Testament except when the preposition is added to a verb to add that meaning. In classical Greek *huper* meant "for," "instead of," "in the name of" (as a representative of another), "because of," and "concerning" (Liddell and Scott). In the New Testament there are four basic ideas expressed by *huper*. (1) It may mean "for" with the sense "in behalf of," especially when used after the verb "pray." Matthew 5:44 is an example of this use: "Pray *for* them which despitefully use you"(author's italics). (2) It can mean "instead of" or "in place of." First Corinthians 15:29, concerning baptism for the dead, is certainly an example of this use. (3) A lesser use of the word is "on account of" or "because of." Acts 5:41 is an example; the disciples rejoiced that they "were counted worthy to suffer shame *for* his name"(author's italics). (4) Finally, *huper* sometimes means "concerning," a meaning synonymous with the preposition *peri*. Second Corinthians 12:8, "For this thing I besought the Lord thrice," is representative of this use.

The first two uses seem to have arisen from the picture

of one person bending over another to shield him, or a shield lifted over the head that takes the blow instead of the person. These two uses of *huper* are sometimes controversial because they often can be interchanged and because they bear upon an all-important truth, "the *vicarious* character of the sacrifice of the death of Christ" (Trench). In passages where Christ is said to have died "for all" or "for us," there arises the question, Does *huper* mean "on behalf of" us, or "in place of" us? (Some of the passages in question are Heb. 2:9; Titus 2:14; 1 Tim. 2:6; Gal. 3:13; Luke 22:19-20; 1 Pet. 2:21; 3:18; 4:1; Rom. 5:8; and John 10:15.) Some would argue that none of these passages speak of Jesus' death as substitutionary, while others would argue that all of them teach substitution, "that Christ suffered, not merely *on our behalf* and *for our good*, but also *in our stead*, and bearing that penalty of our sins which we otherwise must ourselves have borne" (Trench). Further, according to Trench, the majority of passages with *huper* mean no more than "on behalf of" or "for the good of." However, it is certain that *huper* sometimes means "in our stead."

There are examples of this use in secular Greek as well as in the New Testament. In Xenophon's writings the question is found, "Would you die instead of this lad?" (*Anabasis* 7.4-9; also see Plato *Gorgias* 515) Examples are common in the Greek papyri of *huper* used to describe a person writing a letter for (instead of) someone who could not write for himself.[2]

Besides 1 Corinthians 15:29, there are many other cases of *huper* representing the idea of substitution. Paul said that Christ "redeemed us from the curse of the law, being made a curse for us" (Gal. 3:13). He took the place that was rightfully ours. The very same idea is expressed in 2 Corinthians 5:21, "He hath made him to be sin for us."

Concerning Onesimus, Paul wrote to Philemon that he would like to keep him there so that "in your stead he might have ministered unto me" (Philem. 13). Epaphras also was a faithful minister in the stead of the Colossians who could not be present with Paul (Col. 1:7). To the Romans Paul said that he was willing to become accursed before God, to take the place of his brethren, who were estranged from God (Rom. 9:3). Second Corinthians 5:14 obviously speaks of substitution when it says, "Because we thus judge, that if one died for all, then were all dead." Concerning this Colin Brown says, "The death of Christ was the death of all, because he was dying their death."[3] If the idea, one instead of many, is clearly set forth in verse 14, then it is probable that the same idea is meant in verses 15 and 21. Moreover, verse 20 of the same chapter speaks of Paul's beseeching believers "in Christ's stead." Other passages that also may be understood as representing the idea of "in place of" are Romans 8:32; John 10:15; 11:50; 1 Peter 3:18; and 2 Corinthians 5:20.

It may be concluded that when *huper* "expresses some advantage or favor that accrues to persons, its sense is 'on behalf of' (representation) or 'in the place of' (substitution). . . . To act on behalf of a person often involves acting in his place."[4] That is why it is so difficult to separate the two meanings and be certain which is meant because they are so closely related. Some may argue that *huper* should signify only representation because the preposition *anti* signifies substitution. Yet it is not uncommon for prepositions to overlap in meaning. It is also true that a substitute represents someone, and a representative may be a substitute, so it may be concluded that the idea of substitution, while not always the main thrust of *huper*, is never very far away.

The Whole World

One of the key verses on the subject of the extent of the atonement of Christ is 1 John 2:2, which says: "And he is the propitiation for our sins: and not for ours only, but also for the sins of the whole world." At issue is just what is meant by the term "world." In order to answer this question, let us examine the usage of the Greek word *kosmos*. It is used more than one hundred times just in the writings of John, and in every case in the New Testament except one it is translated by the English word *world*. In that one exception it is translated "adorning" in 1 Peter 3:3.

In classical Greek *kosmos* meant "order," in the sense of something being arranged according to a plan. Hence, the phrase *kata kosmon* (according to world) meant "in order." Some argue that prior to this it meant "ornament," "adorning," or "decoration" and that it came to mean "order" because of the beauty there is in arrangements. Whichever came first, both uses of the word were common in classical times. *Kosmos* was used in the second sense especially in reference to the adorning of women (*Iliad* 14.187; Herodotus 5.92). Pythagoras is credited by some as being the first to use *kosmos* to denote the "world-order," but it is more likely that his use of it applied to the order of the whole universe. Finally, it came to mean the "known or inhabited earth" (Liddell and Scott). It is very close in meaning here to the word *oikoumene,* which means "the inhabited world" and sometimes, its inhabitants.

In the secular Greek of the New Testament period many illustrations of the word *kosmos* have been found. A manuscript dated about 9 B.C. says that the birthday of the emperor Augustus is good news to the world. The emperor

Nero is spoken of as "Lord of the whole world." The plural form *kosmois* is used in a third-century document to refer to the "heavens." Examples are also extant that demonstrate the use of the word as "adornment." In 311 B.C. and A.D. 214 the term "womanly kosmos" meant "womanly adornment." Planting a vineyard in an orderly arrangement was called the "*kosmon* (order) of the places."

In the New Testament *kosmos* is used only once with the meaning "ornament." First Peter 3:3, speaking of women, says, "Whose adorning let it not be that outward adorning of plaiting the hair, and of wearing of gold, or of putting on of apparel." This meaning is the common one of *kosmos* in the Old Testament (where the stars are often described as the ornaments of heaven [Deut. 17:3]). At least once *kosmos* is used to refer to the entire universe. Romans 1:20 says, "For the invisible things of him from the creation of the world [*kosmos*] are clearly seen." Another possible reference to the universe is Acts 17:24. More often *kosmos* is limited to the world of the earth. John said the world could not contain the books if all the things Jesus said were recorded (John 21:25). The promise to Abraham was that he should be "heir of the world" (Rom. 4:13). It is used in contrast to spiritual or heavenly things in 1 John 3:17 in the phrase, "whoever has this world's goods."

In addition to these aforementioned meanings, *kosmos* may refer not only to the earth but to its inhabitants, the human race. In Romans 11:12,15 *kosmos* refers to the Gentiles as opposed to the Jews. Believers are spoken of as the light of the world (Matt. 5:14). Often *kosmos* is limited to unregenerate humankind. First John 3:13 says, "Marvel not, my brethren, if the world hate you." Jesus said, "The world cannot hate you; but me it hates because I testify of it, that the works thereof are evil" (John 7:7). From this, *kosmos* sometimes includes not only men in opposition to

God, but their systems of thought and behavior, which are also in opposition to the life of God. An example is Colossians 2:8: "Beware lest any man spoil you through philosophy and vain deceit, after the tradition of men, after the rudiments of the world, and not after Christ."

Finally, *kosmos* may refer not only to the earth, but anything that is part of it. The "things" of the world or, at least, the love of them, is in contrast to spiritual things and love of God. "What shall it profit a man, if he shall gain the whole world, and lose his own soul?" (Mark 8:36). "Love not the world, neither the things that are in the world. If any man love the world, the love of the Father is not in him" (1 John 2:15). Wuest sums up *kosmos* in this way, "*kosmos* is regarded as that order of things whose center is man, attention is directed chiefly to him, and *kosmos* denotes mankind within that order of things, humanity as it manifests itself in and through such an order."[5]

If all of this is applied to the passage mentioned at the beginning of this discussion, 1 John 2:2, it is clear that when it says Jesus was the "propitiation" for the sins of the "whole world," it means everyone on this planet, not just a limited few. Whenever *kosmos* is limited to less than all people, it always refers to those in opposition to God, the unregenerate world, of which we were all a part, at one time. So, to conclude that Jesus died only for the elect few would be to use *kosmos* in a manner that is the opposite of its meaning everywhere else in the New Testament.

One concluding note concerns *kosmos* and its relation to another word that is sometimes translated "world," the word *aion* (age). Like *kosmos*, it has a primary meaning that is physical and a secondary ethical sense. First, it signifies time in its duration, whether long or short. It is the measure of our existence. Ethically, it represents the "spirit or genius of the age" (Trench). In the New Testament "this age" is contrasted with "the coming age" (Matt. 12:32); therefore, it obtains an unfavorable meaning. Trench describes it as

> All that floating mass of thoughts, opinions, maxims, speculations, hopes, impulses, aims, aspirations, at any time current in the world, which it may be impossible to seize and accurately define, but which constitute a most real and effective power, being the moral, or immoral atmosphere which at every moment of our lives we inhale.

Again, it is "the subtle informing spirit of the *kosmos*, or world of men who are living alienated and apart from God."

Chapter 3
The Basis for Salvation

Atonement

The word *atonement* occurs only once in the King James New Testament and not at all in more modern translations. It occurs in Romans 5:11: "But we also joy in God through our Lord Jesus Christ, by whom we have now received the atonement." The Greek word used in this text is *katallage,* which in other texts is translated *reconciliation* (Rom. 11:15; 2 Cor. 5:18-19). The classical meaning of the verb form of the word is "to bring together again people who have been estranged." The noun form would describe the state of those who have been restored to friendship. In the New Testament it refers, of course, to God's reconciling of the world to Himself through the work of Jesus Christ on the cross. Thayer describes it as "the restoration of the favor of God to sinners that repent and put their trust in the expiatory death of Christ."

The English word *atonement* originally represented a harmonious relationship, to be at one with someone, or to be reconciled. However, in modern theological usage the word is used to refer to the process by which this state of harmony is achieved more than to the relationship itself. The Bible assumes that because of sin there is need for atonement if people are to be right with God. The Old Testament speaks often of this need for atonement. The annual sacrifice on what was known as the Day of Atonement was for this purpose (Lev. 16). Although none of the Old Testament sacrifices could remove sin, they do testify to the fact that sin has destroyed fellowship between God and humanity and they point to the death of Christ, the true Lamb of God, who *is* able to take away sin. It is in His sacrifice that their purpose is finally fulfilled. The New Testament word that most corresponds to the Old Testament concept of atonement is *hilaskomai* (to make propitiation) and its other forms, *hilasterion* (place of propitiation), and *hilasmos* (propitiation). See Leviticus 1:4; 4:20,26,31,35;5:10,16,18; 9:7; 14:20; 16:24; 25:9; Numbers 5:8; 1 Chronicles 28:20; Psalm 130:4; and Ezekiel 44:27; 45:15,17 for examples. For further discussion, see the articles on "Propitiation" and "Reconciliation."

The Gospel

The word *euaggelion* means "gospel" or "good news." It occurs seventy-two times in the New Testament; of these fifty-four are in Paul's Epistles. In secular Greek the word referred to a reward for good tidings. It is used in this same manner in the Greek Old Testament. When the messenger came to inform David of the death of Saul and his sons, he expected a reward for what he considered good tidings. However, David had him executed (2 Sam. 4:10). In pagan literature *euaggelion* occasionally refers to a "sac-

rifice offered to celebrate good news." And, finally, it
came to mean "the good news" itself. A reference from
Roman history is the one regarding the birthday of Emperor Augustus (ca. 9 B.C.), which said, "but the birthday
of the god was for the world the beginning of tidings of joy
on his account."

In the New Testament "gospel" is used in its generic
sense to mean "good news." It sums up the whole Christian message. Mark 1:1, for example, says, "The beginning of the gospel of Jesus Christ, the Son of God." The
reference may refer to the gospel that belongs to Jesus
Christ or the good news about Jesus Christ. In this case it
almost certainly refers to the entire history of Jesus' public
ministry, not only to the message preached by Him. The
early church evidently understood it this way because by
the second century the term "gospel" was used to desig-
nate a book giving both the story of Jesus as well as His
message.

The word *gospel* is also used in a more limited sense to
refer to the basic facts included in the message of salvation. W. E. Vine says that Paul used it of two distinct
things: "The basic facts of the death, burial and resurrection of Christ" and "the interpretation of these facts."
Discussing Paul's use of "gospel" Kittel cites 1 Corinthians 9:14, where the noun "gospel" and the verb "proclaim" are used together, and concludes that the phrase
kataggellein to euaggelion can only refer to the content of the
Gospel." The same combination of noun and verb also
occurs in 1 Corinthians 9:18.

Piper observes that Matthew "differentiates between
Jesus' teaching and healing, on the one hand, and his pro-
claiming the gospel, on the other (Matt. 4:23; 9:35; cf.
Luke 9:2; perhaps also Luke 20:21)."[1] Another observation by Piper is very important, the fact that *kerugma* (proc-

lamation) and gospel can be interchanged. He says, "The specific mode of communication implied in *euaggelizesthai* is best brought to light by the two synonyms *kerussein* and *kataggelein,* and by the interchangeable use of *kerugma* ('proclamation') and 'gospel.' "[2] Some argue that the gospel cannot be reduced to a statement of propositional truth. However, there is little doubt left by the New Testament writers that it did consist of a content that could both be defined and recorded.

Many other Scriptures indicate that the gospel, in its most specific sense, represents a message that can be identified, stated, and believed. Ephesians 1:13 says, "In whom you also trusted, after that you heard the word of truth, the gospel of your salvation." Both here and in Colossians 1:5 this description of "gospel" is given. *"Logos* (word) of truth" may be interpreted as the "outward form by which the inward thought is expressed or made known" (Wuest). In 2 Timothy 2:8, Paul identified his "gospel" with the resurrection and Jesus as the Messiah of the line of David. Paul reminded the Corinthians of the "gospel" that he preached, told them to keep it in memory, and then proceeded to define it in the rest of the chapter (1 Cor. 15). This seems to demand the conclusion that the gospel has a specific content. Not only this, Paul opposed the false teachers in Galatia so that the "truth of the gospel" might continue with them (Gal. 2:5,14). He pronounced "anathemas" on anyone who preaches any other gospel than the one true message (Gal. 1:6-9). There is only one gospel, and Jesus is the central figure in it.

There are many ways to present the gospel, but the basic facts contained therein do not differ. From Paul's account of the gospel in 1 Corinthians 15 and the apostolic sermons in Acts, several things become apparent. The most obvious is that the central fact of the gospel is the

death, burial, and resurrection of Christ. Numerous passages confirm this conclusion. One of the most pointed of
these is Acts 4:10: "Be it known unto you all, and to all the
people of Israel, that by the name of Jesus Christ of Naza-
reth, whom you crucified, whom God raised from the
dead, by him does this man stand here before you whole."
Other references include Acts 2:23-24,36; 3:13-15,26;
4:10,33; 5:30; 10:39-40; and 1 Corinthians 15:3,12-17.
Another fact about Jesus that Paul included in his presentation of the gospel is the return of Christ, which will be
the signal for the resurrection of those who believe in Him
(1 Cor. 15:24,35-54). The coming of Christ is also included in Peter's sermon to the Jews in Acts 3:12-26. He said,
"And he shall send Jesus Christ . . . Whom the heaven
must receive until the times of restitution of all things"
(Acts 3:20-21).

A second truth that is emphasized is the fact that all of
these events surrounding Jesus' death, burial, and resurrection took place according to Scripture. They were the
fulfillment of prophecy. Paul said that he delivered
(preached) to them, first of all, "that Christ died for our
sins according to the scriptures" (1 Cor. 15:3). The sermons in Acts also emphasize the importance of this truth.
Other references include Acts 2:16ff.; 3:18,22-25; 4:11;
10:43; 13:23,27,29,33-36; and 26:22.

A third point that is emphasized is that the apostles
were eyewitnesses to the facts of the gospel, which are the
death, burial, and resurrection of Jesus for our sins, as
well as the promise of His return. Peter said, "This Jesus
hath God raised up, whereof we all are witnesses" (Acts
2:32). Paul went to great lengths to show that these facts
were sure, having been witnessed by many, with over five
hundred able to testify of the resurrection (1 Cor. 15:5-
8,15). Other references include Acts 3:15; 4:20,33; 5:32;

10:39-41; 13:31; and 26:16,22.

Finally, the presentation of the "gospel" includes an offer of forgiveness through repentance and faith in Jesus. Peter issued a call to repentance at the conclusion of his sermon at Pentecost (Acts 2:38). After the healing of the lame man he said, "Repent therefore, and be converted, that your sins may be blotted out" (Acts 3:19). Other references include Acts 5:31; 8:22; 10:43; and 13:38-39 (see Acts 26:23 also).

In addition to the definition and the content of the gospel, let us now look at the gospel as it relates to humankind.

1. *The gospel is intended for everyone.* Mark 13:10 says, "The gospel must first be published among all nations." Peter concluded that God has decided that the Gentiles, everyone who is not a Jew, as well as the Jews "should hear the word of the gospel, and believe" (Acts 15:7). (See Mark 16:15 also.)

2. *The gospel is not a human discovery.* Paul declared that the gospel he preached "is not after man." It was given "by the revelation of Jesus Christ" (Gal. 1:11-12). That is why Paul called it the "gospel of God" (1 Thess. 2:2,8,9). Humans did not learn of it by investigation, but we are the beneficiaries of God's revelation.

3. *The gospel is something that must be believed and received.* Jesus Himself declared, "The kingdom of God is at hand: repent ye, and believe the gospel" (Mark 1:15). Receiving and accepting the gospel are mentioned by Paul in his letter to the Corinthians (2 Cor. 11:4).

4. *The gospel is such that if you know it you must proclaim it.* Paul's desire was to "preach the gospel in the regions beyond" (2 Cor. 10:16). He described it as a "necessity" that was laid upon him. He said, "Woe is unto me, if I preach not the gospel" (1 Cor. 9:16). Mark 16:15, though a dis-

puted passage, records a command to "preach the gospel to every creature." Every believer is to testify of the gospel of the grace of God (Acts 1:8).

5. *Though the gospel is God's, He entrusts it to human beings.* Paul said that "we were allowed of God to be put in trust with the gospel" (1 Thess. 2:4). Because of this we are accountable to God rather than individuals. Deacons are to be those who hold as they would a treasure the mystery of the faith with a pure conscience (1 Tim. 3:9). The treasure of the gospel is spoken of as being housed in earthen (human) vessels (2 Cor. 4:3,7).

6. *Jesus said that people must be willing to give up everything for the sake of the gospel (Mark 10:29).* They must have enough faith in the gospel to risk all for it (Mark 8:35). They must be like Paul who "suffered the loss of all things" for the excellency of the knowledge of Christ (Phil. 3:8).

7. *The gospel may be served.* Paul described himself as a "servant of Jesus Christ" who is "separated unto the gospel" (Rom. 1:1). He was one who "ministers," speaking of temple service, the gospel (Rom. 15:16). Timothy served with Paul "in the gospel" (Phil. 2:22), as also the women mentioned by Paul (4:3).

8. *The gospel can be defended.* During his imprisonment Paul said that he was set for the "defense of the gospel" (Rom. 1:17, see also v. 7).

9. *On the negative side, it is also possible to hinder the gospel.* Paul did not take money from the Corinthians because he was afraid he would be accused of preaching for money and thus hinder the reception of the gospel (1 Cor. 9:12).

10. *The gospel can be rejected.* As Barclay says, "It is the characteristic of love that love can only offer and can never coerce. A man can spurn the offer of God or he can completely disregard it. He can live as if the good news did not exist, but he does so at the peril of his immortal

soul."[3] Paul said that when Jesus comes, He will take vengeance on those who "obey not the gospel of our Lord Jesus Christ" (2 Thess. 1:8). Other references include Romans 10:16 and 1 Peter 4:17.

11. *Finally, it is possible for a person to pervert the gospel.* Paul warned the Galatians that there were some who would "pervert the gospel of Christ" (Gal. 1:7). Any form of gospel than that found in the Scriptures is "another" gospel and is denounced by the apostle. "When a man begins to believe in or seek to propagate Christianity as he would like it to be instead of as God proclaims it is," he is perverting the gospel of Christ.[4]

Propitiation

The word *propitiation* is found three times in the *King James Version* of the New Testament. The noun form of the Greek word (*hilasmos*) is found in 1 John 2:2 ("He is the propitiation for our sins: and not for ours only, but also for the . . . whole world") and 1 John 4:10 ("Herein is love, not that we loved God, but that he loved us, and sent his Son to be the propitiation for our sins") The adjectival form (*hilasterion*), which is sometimes used as a noun, is also translated "propitiation" in Romans 3:25 ("whom God hath set forth to be a propitiation through faith in his blood"). In Hebrews 9:5 *hilasterion* is used to refer to the "mercy seat" in the Old Testament tabernacle. The verb form (*hilaskomai*) also occurs twice. In Luke 18:13 the publican prayed, "God be merciful to me a sinner." Hebrews 2:17 says that Jesus was a merciful high priest "to make reconciliation for the sins of the people."

In Greek literature all three of these words mean to *propitiate*. They are used in connection with the rites of pagan religions. The verb form means to "appease" and is always used in reference to pagan gods (Homer, *Odyssey* 3.419). *Hilasterion* referred to a propitiatory sacrifice, and *hilasmos* denoted "a means of appeasing" (Plutarch *Sol.* 12). Pagans offered a sacrifice as a means of appeasing the anger of their god. In addition, there are several examples in the Greek world of the word *hilasterion* denoting a monument erected to honor a deity. An inscription has been found on the island of Cos that mentions a "votive gift which the people of Cos erected as a *hilasterion* for the welfare of the Emperor Augustus" (Moulton and Milligan).

R. Abba, in the *Interpreter's Dictionary of the Bible*, states that *hilaskomai* in secular Greek means to "propitiate," but points out that it also has "a rare secondary meaning of 'to expiate.'" He then argues that the primary sense of this family of words in the Greek Old Testament (Septuagint) is "expiation" and that their use in the Septuagint to express "propitiation" is "rare and exceptional." He then argues that the meaning of *hilasterion* and *hilasmos* in the New Testament is derived from their use in the Old Testament, "where they have the general sense of 'expiation' and do not as religious terms bear the meaning of 'propitiating God.'" He says that the idea of propitiation is "not prominent in the Old Testament." It expresses "pagan conceptions of appeasing the Deity and is inappropriate to the religion of Israel."[5]

Now the word *expiate* means "to remove guilt by the suffering of a penalty," "to make satisfaction for," or "to make atonement." It is obvious that the words in question mean this much at least. In Leviticus 25:9 *hilasmos* refers to the Day of Atonement, and in Numbers 5:8 it refers to a sacrifice of atonement. The question is whether or not it is proper to use the stronger term propitiation in reference to God. Abba has admitted that the Greek world used these terms with the idea of "propitiation" in mind.[6] It would then be dangerous for Paul to use such terms in the Greek world, which he did, without running the risk of their being understood as denoting "propitiation" in some sense. In addition, he made no attempt to avoid such an understanding by explaining them otherwise. Moreover, it also has been admitted that while the idea of propitiation is not prominent in the Old Testament (some would say it *is* prominent), it does occur. If it occurs at all, it must be dealt with, so the frequency of its occurrence is a moot point. So then what does "propitiation" mean? In the Christian context the thought is not of placating the anger of a wrathful God, but of satisfying the demands of His righteous nature, "so that His government might be maintained, and that mercy might be shown on the basis of justice duly satisfied" (Wuest). This is explained very clearly in Romans 3:25-26: "Whom God hath set forth to be a propitiation through faith in his blood . . . To declare, I say, at this time his righteousness: that he might be just, and the justifier of him which believes in Jesus." God's righteousness had to be satisfied in a manner by which He could both forgive sin and still be just. His plan for accomplishing this was given ahead of time in Isaiah 53:11: "He shall see the travail of his soul, and shall be satisfied." He could not simply forgive sin without sacrifice for sin (Heb. 9:17).

Another difference between the pagan concept of God and biblical teaching about God is that He is always the same. He is immutable, but His relative attitude does change toward those who come to Him in faith. He can act differently towards them on the ground of the propitiatory sacrifice of Christ, "not because He has changed, but because He ever acts according to His unchanging righteousness" (Vine).

Still, there are those who argue that the idea of propitiation does not occur in the New Testament. One may agree
that the pagan idea does not occur in the New Testament,
but it has already been shown that the sanctified version of
propitiation does occur in Romans 3:25-26 (see 1 John
2:2; 4:10 also). The real question is whether or not the
righteousness of God demands satisfaction for sin. The
New Testament is very clear that it does. All of the terms
that speak of Christ as a sacrifice or an offering for sin are
proof of the fact. Ephesians 5:2 says that Jesus gave Himself as "an offering and a sacrifice to God for a sweet-
smelling savor." He is "our passover," "sacrificed for us"
(1 Cor. 5:7). He is the Lamb of God (John 1:29,36; 1 Pet.
1:19). Even more pointed are those passages that describe
Him as washing us in His blood (see Rev. 1:5).

There are those who reject the concept of propitiation
and translate *hilasmos* and *hilasterion* with the word *expiation*. For example, Abba says, "There is no idea in the NT
of the wrath of God being propitiated by the sacrifice of
Christ. It is God in Christ who reconciles the world to
Himself (2 Cor. 5:19)."[7] The idea of reconciliation is certainly a New Testament concept. However, to make such a
statement is to imply that reconciliation (*katallage*) and
propitiation (*hilasterion*) are synonyms, which they obviously are not. As Trench points out, reconciliation declares that we were enemies of God and by the death of
Christ were made friends of God, but "how made friends
Katallage would not describe at all. It would not of itself,
necessarily imply satisfaction, propitiation, the Daysman,
the Mediator, the High Priest; all which in *hilasmos* are involved." In *katallage* man is reconciled to God; in *hilasterion*
God's righteousness is satisfied.

A final note on the word *hilasterion* concerns the question of whether or not it also can be translated "mercy

seat" rather than "propitiation." The question arises because the word is used in the Septuagint to translate the
Hebrew term for mercy seat (Ex. 25:16-17), and in Hebrews 9:5 it is used to denote the mercy seat also. However, Deissmann is probably correct in his conclusion that
hilasterion is not an exact rendering for "mercy seat," but
should more properly be translated the "propitiatory article."[8] The translation "mercy seat" would not be a proper
translation for *hilasterion* in Romans 3:25 because the emphasis there is not on the place but the satisfactory offering that was made for sin.

Chapter 4
The Application of Salvation

The Gift of God

Salvation is described as the gift of God in Ephesians 2:8. As such it is in accordance with grace and is totally apart from works: "not of works, lest any man should boast" (v. 9). Salvation is a gift that originates with God and comes to humanity complete, with nothing needed to be added. Persons are simply to receive the gift of faith. The Greek word that is used to denote this gift is *doron*, which means "a gift" or "present."

Doron is from the same root as the verb *didomi*, which occurs 416 times in the New Testament. It has several other kindred terms. The verb form *doreomai* (present) is another derivation of the same word. Also corresponding to it is the older form *dorema* (present) and *dorea* (a present or gift). It is interesting that the accusative form *dorean* is used as an adverb to describe something undeservedly free.

In classical Greek literature *doron* "denotes especially a

complimentary gift."[1] It is also used to denote a gift or a dispensation from the gods. Conversely, it may refer to a gift or offering brought by men to God. Other meanings include a tax, tribute, or bribe. In the secular papyruses of the New Testament period, it is commonly used for a sacrifice to a god or an offering to the temple treasury. Presents from one person to another are also described by *doron*. Moulton and Milligan mention an interesting example of a thank-you note that says, "It was good of you, you sent me a present, such a beauty—just husks!"

The Greek Old Testament uses *doron* to translate several different Hebrew words. (1) It refers to gifts from one person to another. Jacob gave a present to his brother Esau (Gen. 32:13). (2) In Judges 3:15 and 17 *doron* denotes the tribute that Eglon, king of Moab, forced Israel to give to him. (3) In Deuteronomy 16:19, judges were forbidden to take bribes (gifts) lest justice be perverted. (4) The most common use of *doron* in the Old Testament is to denote offerings given to the Lord (Lev. 1:2,10,14; 2:1). (5) Finally, it may refer to a gift from God (Gen. 30:20). Leah said that God had endowed her with a good dowry, her six sons.

The kindred term *dorea* occurs only in the adverbial form *dorean* in the Old Testament. It most often means "without payment" or "without cause." David would not make an offering to the Lord that cost him nothing (2 Sam. 24:24). Saul wanted to slay David without cause (1 Sam. 19:5).

In the New Testament *doron* occurs nineteen times. Once it is used to describe gifts exchanged between human beings. In another case it describes the gift of adoration that the wise men brought to Jesus (Matt. 2:11). Generally, it is used to denote a sacrifice or offering given to God. Matthew 5:23; Luke 21:1; and Hebrews 5:1 are examples of this use. Only once is it used to refer to the divine gift of salvation (Eph. 2:8). The usual word for a divine gift to humans is *dorea*. Jesus spoke of the "gift of God" in His encounter with the Samaritan woman (John 4:10). *Dorea* describes the gift of the Holy Spirit (Acts 2:38); the gift of righteousness (Rom. 5:15,17; 5:16 uses *dorema*); the unspeakable gift, which is probably Christ Himself (2 Cor. 9:15); grace gifts (Eph. 4:7); and the heavenly gift (Heb. 6:4).

Thayer makes a distinction between these two phrases: *dorean theou* (gift of God) refers to an expression of His favor; *doron theou* (gift of God) refers to something that becomes the recipient's abiding possession. Whether this distinction can always be made between the two is open to question; however, it does appear to be generally the case.

The word that most clearly underlines the free and unmerited nature of God's gifts is the adverb *dorean*. Eight times it occurs in the New Testament. Six times it means that something is given "for nothing" or "gratis." Jesus instructed the Twelve as they went out on their mission: "freely you have received, freely give" (Matt. 10:8). Paul said that we are "justified freely by his grace" (Rom. 3:24). Twice Paul said he labored with his own hands so that the gospel might be without charge (2 Cor. 11:7; 2 Thess. 3:8). Twice Jesus said in Revelation that whoever is thirsty may take the "water of life freely" (Rev. 21:6; 22:17). In John 15:25 *dorean* means "without cause," and in Galatians 2:21 it means "for nothing" or "in vain."

God's gifts to us are prominent in the New Testament. He has given us eternal life (John 10:28). He has given us the gift of the Holy Spirit (Acts 2:38). He has given spiritual gifts for the carrying on of the work of the church (Eph. 4:8,11-12). But the greatest gift is the Unspeakable One Himself (2 Cor. 9:15). He has given His "only begotten Son" for us (John 3:16). All He wants of us who have received the gift of eternal life is that we offer ourselves to Him (Rom. 12:1-2; 2 Cor. 8:5). This is the "only legitimate 'offering' which can and should be brought by men to God."[2]

Repentance

While preaching in Galilee, Jesus addressed the question of whether or not a group of Galileans who were murdered by Pilate were greater sinners than anyone else because they suffered such a fate. He said, "I tell you, No: but, except you repent, you shall all likewise perish" (Luke 13:1-3). Both John the Baptist and Jesus preached, "Repent ye: for the kingdom of heaven is at hand" (Matt. 3:2; 4:17). Just what did Jesus mean when He said, "Repent"? The Greek word He used is *metanoeo*, which is a combination of the words *meta* (after) and *noeo* (to understand or perceive). So, literally, the noun form *metanoia* (repentance) means an "afterthought" or "change of mind." The most important question, however, is, does repentance consist entirely of a mental exercise or does it imply more than that?

On one hand, there are those who insist that repentance cannot involve anything more than a change of mind or attitude toward God; otherwise, they contend it would negate the doctrine of salvation by grace. It cannot be understood as a condition of salvation unless it is concluded that repentance is only a "synonym for faith."[3] Obviously, when people move from unbelief to faith in Christ, they have changed their minds, which constitutes repentance. It is argued that "repentance does not mean to turn from sin, nor a change in one's conduct."[4] It does not mean to change one's life because that would constitute works.

On the other hand, many others believe that repentance involves more. W. E. Vine says, "In the New Testament the subject chiefly has reference to repentance from sin, and this change of mind involves both a turning from sin and a turning to God." Thayer, in his lexicon, defines *metanoia* as "esp. the change of mind of those who have begun to abhor their errors and misdeeds, and have determined to enter upon a better course of life, so that it embraces both a recognition of sin and sorrow for it." Moulton and Milligan in their work on Greek vocabulary conclude concerning *metanoeo*: "Its meaning deepens with Christianity, and in the New Testament it is more than 'repent,' and indicates a complete change of attitude, spiritual and moral, towards God." Trench says that *metonoia* is "the expression of the nobler repentance." He lists four ideas that are included in the meaning of repentance: (1) it means to know (perceive) afterwards; (2) it signifies the change of mind that comes as a result of this knowledge; (3) it involves regret for the course pursued (displeasure at one's own self); and (4) it signifies a change of conduct for the future based on this change of mind. In addition to these, Kenneth Wuest explains that *metanoia*

> includes not only the act of changing one's attitude towards and opinion of sin but also that of forsaking it. Sorrow and contrition with respect to sin, are included in the Bible idea of repentance. . . . The emotional and volitional aspects of the act of repentance follow, and are the result of this intellectual process of a change of mind with respect to it.

Those who believe that repentance includes forsaking of sin are accused by those who do not accept that view of teaching a "works salvation," a denial of the doctrine of grace. On the other hand, those who teach that repentance is simply a "change of mind about who Christ is" are charged with teaching an "easy believism." About this view John MacArthur says, "It is utterly devoid of any recognition of personal guilt, any intent to obey God, or any desire for true righteousness."[5]

In order to determine who is right, there are several questions that should be explored. First, does repentance necessarily involve sorrow for sin? Second Corinthians 7:10 says, "For godly sorrow worketh repentance to salvation not to be repented of: but the sorrow of the world worketh death." Strictly speaking, sorrow and repentance are different entities, because people may have sorrow without repentance. However, can people have repentance without sorrow? "Godly sorrow leads to repentance." Would persons desire to be saved without first realizing they are sinners and lost? Before realizing that fact they may be quite happy in their sin. After being convicted by the Holy Spirit that they are sinners and as a result lost, can they desire to be saved (go to heaven), put their faith and trust in Christ for eternal life, and still be happy about their life of sin? Can people be repentant toward God and unrepentant toward sin and self? The answer is, people could if God would let them. But the same Holy Spirit who causes persons to see the error of their ways and desire to come to Christ is the One who convicts the world of sin, of righteousness, and of judgment. If the Spirit truly convicts people of sin, it would be impossible for them not to have a changed attitude toward their sin, a sense of sorrow at having sinned against God. That change is called repentance.

Another question that should be asked is, What does repentance toward God involve? Does it involve receiving Jesus as Savior only, or must one acknowledge Him as

Lord also? It is argued by some that it is necessary to receive Jesus as Savior only in order to be saved. However, several Scriptures seem to indicate that the two ideas go together. Acts 16:31 says, "Believe on the Lord Jesus Christ and you shall be saved." Romans 10:9 says, "That if you shall confess with your mouth the Lord Jesus, and shall believe in your heart that God has raised him from the dead, you shall be saved." Peter declared at Pentecost "that God has made that same Jesus, whom you have crucified, both Lord and Christ" (Acts 2:36). Some argue that this use of the word "Lord" simply means to acknowledge that Jesus is God. Yet, if He be God, then He is certainly Lord. Persons do not have to "make Jesus Lord" because He is Lord. What it does mean is that when individuals repent in their attitude toward Jesus, they are changing from unbelief to faith in two facts: (1) that Jesus is who He claims to be—Lord and God; and (2) that He in fact did what He said He would do—die for our sins on the cross and offer us forgiveness based on that sacrifice. The rest of the Christian life, then, is the struggle to practice daily what we have professed at the beginning. Since Jesus is Lord, believers are to allow Him to be Lord of their lives.

The final question concerning the meaning of repentance is, What affect does it have on the will? Can people put their faith in Christ and never intend to make any change in the direction of their life? It is obvious that the changes in life-style are the fruits of repentance and come as a result, not a cause of salvation. However, what about intentions? One thing is sure: this decision is not a presalvation work that is required to set life in order so persons can be saved. Such an attempt at self-reformation is not true repentance. It involves trusting one's own works instead of Christ's. But can individuals trust Christ as Savior and never have any intention to change the direction of their lives? To put it another way, can people be true believers in Christ and not followers of Christ?

There are three lines of evidence that indicate it is not possible to do so. First, there is the evidence from the ministry of Jesus. In His dealing with people who came to Him, He never offered anything less than a new way of life. One very clear example is that of the rich young ruler. He wanted to know what to do "to inherit eternal life" (Luke 18:18). Jesus answered, "One thing you lack. Sell all that you have, and distribute unto the poor, . . . and come, follow me." The man refused to do so, but Jesus made no other offer to the man. The parable of the two sons demonstrates that it is not what people profess but what they actually do that counts. One son said he would obey his father, but did not. The other refused, but later repented and did the will of his father (Matt. 21:28-31).

Another line of evidence is that found in 2 Corinthians 5:17: "Therefore if any man be in Christ, he is a new creature: old things are passed away; behold, all things are become new." The point is, people cannot be saved without being changed from the inside out. They do not change themselves; it is God who recreates persons. This work of God in believers' lives leads us to a third line of evidence, the fruit of repentance. If people have truly believed and been converted, there must be evidence of a new life. John the Baptist demanded fruits of repentance (Luke 3:8ff.). John also said that this is how we know that we know Christ, "if we keep His commandments" (1 John 2:3). (See Gal. 5:21 and James 2:14ff. also.)

Because of this, it must be concluded that repentance also involves the decision to make a radical change in the direction of our lives. It represents a new departure, the beginning point of a different attitude toward life. The new purpose is to become a follower of Jesus. The proof of repentance is people's deeds. There is no reason to think people have repented if there has been no change in their lives, because words alone do not save.

Receive

John 1:11-12 says, "He came unto his own, and his own received him not. But as many as received him, to them gave he power to become the sons of God, even to them that believe on his name." Based on this verse is the popular terminology that one needs to "receive Christ as one's Savior." What does it mean to "receive" Christ?

The Greek word for "receive" in John 1:12 is *lambano.* In classical Greek *lambano* has two main uses. One is more active, "to take"; the other is more passive, "to receive." The more active use means to take hold of, grasp, or seize something. Examples of this use include to catch an enemy, seize an opportunity, take in hand or undertake something, apprehend with the mind, or be taken by illness. The more passive meaning is also used in a variety of ways. Examples are to have something given to you (get), receive hospitality (welcome), receive in-laws from a marriage, receive a name, receive punishment, receive profits, or receive permission for something.

In the secular documents of New Testament times similar uses of the word have been compiled by Moulton and Milligan. The uses of *lambano* include: (1) to receive something, such as a document or money; (2) to get or obtain something, such as legal satisfaction; (3) to signify receiving of goods in business transactions; and (4) to take something or someone, such as a captive. An interesting example is a first-century B.C. note by a woman who claimed to have been severely beaten by another woman.

The note from the beaten woman says, "and, if I survive, I may obtain satisfaction from her as is right." Another note says, "If you get any lentils send them to me by Katoitus" (fourth century A.D.).

In the New Testament *lambano* is very common. It occurs 263 times. Of these only a few deal with receiving Christ or the testimony concerning Him. It is used in Mark 4:20 (Matt. 13:20; Luke 8:13 use the synonym *dechomai* in the same context) of those who receive the Word of God. In John 3:11 Jesus said to Nicodemus, "We speak that we do know, and testify that we have seen; and ye receive not our witness." In John 3:32-33 *lambano* is used of receiving the testimony of John the Baptist about Jesus. He explains what it means, "He that hath received his testimony hath set to his seal that God is true. For he whom God hath sent speaketh the words of God" (vv. 33-34). To receive testimony is to accept it as true, to believe it (see John 3:36). To fail to receive His words is the same as rejecting Christ (John 12:48).

Only two times is *lambano* used of receiving Christ. In John 1:11-12, those who "receive" him are equated with those who "believe on his name." Jesus Himself said to the Jews, "I am come in my Father's name, and you receive me not." A few verses later He says, "For had you believed Moses, you would have believed me" (John 5:43,46).

Lambano was not used by Paul; however, he did use the word *paralambano*, which simply adds the prefix *para*. This means "to take to oneself." In 1 Thessalonians 2:13 he used it of receiving the Word of God, and in Colossians 2:6 he used it of receiving Christ: "As ye have therefore received Christ Jesus the Lord, so walk ye in him." Again, receiving is equated with having faith because that is how the believer is to walk and that is how he or she is born again. So, it is clear that in every case where the word to *receive* is used in reference to Christ or His word, it is used as a synonym of "believe" or "have faith."[6]

Faith and Works

One of the fundamental issues in the Christian faith is the relationship between faith and works in relation to salvation. The apostle Paul strongly emphasized that salvation is a gift of God and cannot be earned in any way. Titus 3:5 says, "Not by works of righteousness which we have done, but according to His mercy He saved us." Romans 4:5 says, "But to him that works not, but believes on Him that justifies the ungodly, his faith is counted for righteousness." Again, Ephesians 2:8-9 reads, "For by grace are you saved through faith; and that not of yourselves; it is the gift of God; not of works, lest any man should boast." If then works play no role in obtaining salvation, how does one reconcile the statement of James that "faith, if it has not works, is dead, being alone" (2:17) or "that by works a man is justified, and not by faith only" (v. 24).

To attempt to answer this question, let us first begin with a definition of the word *faith*. The noun form is *pistis* (faith) and the verb form is *pisteuo* (believe). These are very common terms in the New Testament. For example, *pisteuo* is found twenty-nine times in the Synoptic Gospels and ninety-nine times in the Gospel of John. In secular Greek literature, as well as in the New Testament, faith has two basic meanings. It may denote an intellectual assent or a belief that something is true. O. Michel says that this use arose during the Hellenistic period. During the struggle with skepticism and atheism, it acquired the sense of conviction concerning the existence and activity of the Greek gods.[7] Thayer calls this the intransitive use of the word: to be sure or be persuaded that something is a fact. This kind of faith does not require any action on the part of the believer—only intellectual acceptance. James used this type of faith as an example of a dead faith: "The devils also believe, and tremble" (2:19).

The original meaning that is the more common use of faith in the New Testament is the transitive or active use. It means to "put faith in" or "rely upon" someone or something. Sometimes it has even stronger meaning: "To entrust something to another." In classical usage it denoted conduct that honored a previous agreement, such as the honoring of a truce between opposing armies (*Iliad* 2.124). The meaning of entrusting some thing to someone is found in Xenophon (*Memorabilia* 4.4.17). An example of this use in the New Testament is 2 Timothy 1:12. Paul said, "I know whom I have believed, and am persuaded that he is able to keep that which I have committed unto him against that day." It means to trust in or rely upon Christ to save us.

The question is, Is there a kind of faith that one may have in Christ that is not a saving faith? And then, if there is, how does one tell the difference? Let us look at what James said on this matter. He began the discussion by raising the question, "What does it profit, my brethren, though a man say he has faith, and has not works? can that faith save him?" (Jas. 2:14). There are several reasons that James gave to show a kind of faith does exist that does not save. First, he began by putting the definite article in front of faith (*he pistis*), which has the effect of pointing out a particular kind of faith (that faith) rather than faith in general. A second thing that must be noted is that James was referring to a man who said he had faith (v. 14). Moreover, he put the phrase in the subjunctive, which means that his statement is in the realm of possibility, not reality. He said that he had faith, but whether he really did is still open to question.

Next James gave two examples from the everyday world about response to human need (vv. 15-16). A brother or sister comes in who does not have sufficient clothing or food for the day, and he or she is told to eat and be warmed, but no help is given. That kind of advice, no matter how well meaning, is worthless. The implication is that the kind of faith that causes a person to react in this manner is also worthless.

James went on to say that belief about God is not enough. It is good to believe that God is one (v. 19). This conviction was the cornerstone of Jewish orthodoxy. However, the demons believe this also. But instead of believing the truth and trusting in it, they believe it and "tremble" or "bristle" in reaction to it. So, intellectual faith alone does not bring about a right relationship with God.

Finally, James charged that faith without works has no life to it; it is dead (vv. 17,20). It is like a body without any spirit (or breath) in it; and without the spirit, the body cannot live. It is interesting that faith is compared to the outward, visible person and works are compared to the inner person or the spirit. Two examples of how faith and works are to interact are cited from the Old Testament. The first is Abraham. His faith was made "complete" in his offering of Isaac. The second example is Rahab, the harlot, who risked her life to help the Jewish spies escape from Jericho because she had faith in God. One must notice that these are two very different examples: the father of the Jews and a Gentile harlot. It is obvious that James was not arguing that Abraham was not saved by the offering of Isaac, but Abraham had faith in God and had proved it to the world by his works for most of a lifetime, even before the event mentioned by James. It is also plain, too, that he was not arguing against the Pauline doctrine of justification by faith, because he wrote his epistle before any of Paul's letters were written. So, what was he trying to show? He was simply trying to illustrate the nature of true faith: that faith and deeds are a unity. Faith cannot be separated from works. True faith will always lead to works. Paul taught the same truth in a different way. In Galatians 5:19-23, he spoke of the fruit of the Spirit and the works of the flesh. Those who habitually live in the works of the flesh "shall not inherit the kingdom of God" (v. 21). On this subject, Jesus also gave the parable of the two sons (Matt. 21:28-32). The point of the parable is that the one who pleases his father is not the one who says he will obey, but the one who obeys. The conclusion is faith and works will not contradict each other. They are inexorably related.

Be Converted

After the healing of the lame man at the beautiful gate of the temple, Peter preached to the Jews who were present. In this sermon he exhorted them in the following manner: "Repent ye therefore, and be converted, that your sins may be blotted out" (Acts 3:19). The Greek word for *be converted* is *epistrepho*, which is found thirty-nine times in the New Testament. In six of these cases it is translated by the word *convert*. The word *strepho* is also translated *convert* twice (Matt. 18:3; John 12:40).

In classical Greek *strepho* means to "turn" or "turn about." It is used of causing soldiers to "wheel around." It means to "cause to rotate" as does a potter's wheel upon an axis. It also can mean to "overturn," "change," or "convert" something or someone. The kindred word *epistrepho* is simply *strepho* plus *epi* (a preposition that has the basic meaning "upon"). In this case the preposition does not appreciably change the meaning of the original verb; it only intensifies the meaning of the verb. *Epistrepho* also means to "turn," or "turn about." Like *strepho* it also can mean to "wheel around" as a wild boar upon a hunter who is stalking him. It may mean to "turn toward" something, or to "convert from an error," "correct," or "cause someone to repent." (See Liddell and Scott for other examples.)

In the New Testament *strepho* means to "turn," "change," or "return." It signifies a change in direction. Stephen said that in the wilderness Israel "in their hearts turned back again into Egypt" (Acts 7:39). Because of their false worship, "God turned, and gave them up to worship the host of heaven" (v. 42). It is descriptive of Paul's actions at Antioch of Pisidia when the Jews rejected the Word of God. He said that they judged themselves "unworthy of everlasting life, lo, we turn to the Gentiles" (Acts 13:46). The most interesting use of *strepho* is in Matthew 18:3, which says, "Except you be converted, and become as little children, you shall not enter into the kingdom of heaven." To be saved a person must become as a little child. This may mean that one must have the faith of a child or it may refer to the fact that one must begin anew, or be born again. The implication also is that being saved involves a change in the direction of one's life.

The verb *epistrepho* means to "turn to something," to "cause to return," "turn around," "turn towards," or "convert." The noun form *epistrepho* signifies a "turning around." It is used of the "conversion of the Gentiles" (Acts 15:3). *Epistrepho* denotes how the Thessalonians "turned to God from idols to serve the living and true

God" (1 Thess. 1:9). This action implies both repentance and faith, as well as a life that shows a change of direction. They once served idols, now they serve the "living and true God." This word is used to describe the conversion of the people of Lydda and Saron (Acts 9:35), and at Antioch also, a "great number believed, and turned to the Lord" (11:21). Paul told the people of Lystra that they should "turn from these vanities unto the living God" (14:15). Paul summarized his message to the Gentiles in his defense before King Agrippa, in which he said he showed them "that they should repent and turn to God, and do works meet for repentance" (Acts 26:20).[8]

The question that should be answered in this regard is, Can a person be saved and not be converted? Certainly not. It is clear from these examples that both Jesus and Paul in their preaching demanded a change in those desiring to follow Christ. One could not continue to practice pagan religious rites and be a Christian. There had to be a change of attitude (repentance) toward their former religion—it was necessary for them to see their old pagan religion as worthless and even demonic, and to have a new attitude toward the true God—faith. In addition, it was expected of the new believers that their behavior would show to the world that they had a new direction in life— they had turned around. They had not arrived yet, but they were headed in a different direction. One must remember, however, that these changes are not brought about by human effort or reformation. As W. E. Vine put it, "Divine grace is the efficient cause, human agency the responding effect."

Believe into Jesus

The apostle John spoke often of believing in Jesus. It is interesting that he commonly used the preposition *eis*, which means "into" rather than the preposition *en* (in, on). In fact, he used this combination thirty-three times, and an additional three times he used the phrase "believe on his name" (1:12; see also 2:23; 3:18*b*). The English versions do not make any distinction between the prepositions *en, epis,* and *epi,* which are all used after the verb *pisteuo* (believe). However, there is a subtle difference between them in emphasis. *En* takes the locative case and refers to the sphere within which an action takes place. When individuals believe *in* Christ, the emphasis is that their faith is centered in Christ. They now have a different frame of reference. The preposition *epi* (upon) signifies that the believer's faith is upon Christ. The emphasis is that he is trusting Christ or resting upon Him (Acts 16:31). *Eis* generally is used to denote movement or entry into something. It implies movement (to Christ) that results in a new position (in Christ). Westcott says, "There is the combination (as it were) of rest and motion, of a continuous relation, with a realisation of it."[9] There is implied a coming to Christ and resting in Him, all in that one little word.

The phrase "believe on [*eis*] his name" is even more significant. The name of a person stands for that person and what he or she truly is. Greek papyruses and inscriptions have shed a great deal of light on the meaning of the phrase *eis to onoma* (literally "into the name"). Deissmann says that this phrase is so common in secular Greek that it is often abbreviated to *eis ono.* It became an idiom that meant to "transfer to the name of" or to the account of someone else. He gives an example from an ostracon from his own collection that was found at Thebes and dates from the second century A.D. It is part of an order to an official of the state granary to transfer wheat to another person's account.[10]

The phrase "believe into His name" represents the presentation of an object in relation to its ownership. Slaves were bought for various uses in pagan temples "into the name" of that deity. To "believe into Jesus" would mean to cease being the property of a pagan god and become a possession of the Lord Jesus Christ, transferred into His account.

Confess Jesus

One of the great passages in the New Testament concerning salvation is Romans 10:9-10: "That if you will confess with your mouth the Lord Jesus, and will believe in your heart that God has raised him from the dead, you will be saved. For with the heart man believes unto righteousness; and with the mouth confession is made unto salvation." The role of faith in salvation is well known, but what about "confessing" the "Lord Jesus" or "confessing" that "Jesus is Lord"? What does that mean? Let us begin by looking at the word *confess* (*homologeo*).

The literal meaning of *homologeo* is "to say the same thing" or "to agree with." In secular documents from New Testament times it was commonly used to denote agreements between two parties. In legal formulas it meant to "give consent" to something. Another use of the word was to "acknowledge" or "publicly declare." One papyrus from the first century reads, "He acknowledges [having found] the box, but alleges that it was empty"

(Moulton and Milligan).

The Greek Old Testament uses a compound form of the word *exomologeo* to translate *yadah*, which can mean either "praise" or "confess an offense." This is a strange combination to us, but it is easier to understand in connection when a person in prayer confesses his faults, and the fact that without forgiveness, the punishment that might have come would have been just. One comes to the point where he/she praises God in the whole matter. An example of this is found in Joshua 7:19, where Joshua counseled Achan to give "glory to the Lord God of Israel, and make confession unto him." He was asked to do this just before his execution.

Homologeo occurs twenty-six times in the New Testament; the noun form (confession) six times; and *exomologeo* ten times. It has several related meanings in the New Testament. (1) It means to agree with or concede something. In Hebrews 11:13, the patriarchs are said to have "confessed that they were strangers and pilgrims on the earth." (2) The most frequent use of *homologeo* is to denote confession of guilt either to God or to men. First John 1:9 speaks of confession (saying the same thing that God does) of sin. The people of Ephesus who believed also confessed their deeds (Acts 19:18). (3) Several times this word denotes to "make a promise." Herod "promised with an oath" to give John the Baptist's head to Salome (Matt. 14:7). Judas made a promise to betray Jesus (Luke 22:6; see Acts 17:7 also). (4) The Old Testament use of *homologeo* is a sacrifice of praise to God. Hebrews 13:15 says, "Therefore by him let us continually offer the sacrifice of praise to God, that is, the fruit of our lips giving thanks [*homologounton*] to his name." (5) Finally, "confess" may refer to a profession of faith, an open declaration that one is a follower of Christ. Romans 10:9-10 and Matthew

10:32-33 are examples of this usage. When people make this confession, there is a sense in which they are also doing all of the other things denoted by *homologeo*.

Romans 10:9-10 declares that God wants us to make a confession with the mouth. The confession is, "Jesus is Lord." Moreover, we are to believe in our hearts that God raised Jesus from the dead. The import of this verse is to say that true faith will lead to confession (profession) of Christ. Luther said that such confession is "the principal work of faith." Calvin added that no one can believe with the heart without confessing with the mouth. It is a natural consequence of faith. But there is a great deal of controversy among evangelicals concerning what the confession "Jesus is Lord" implies.

On one side of the issue, there are those who separate from the gospel message anything that sounds like a work of righteousness. Their motivation is to keep the gospel pure from the encroachment of human works. The belief of this group is to separate the "objective aspect of Jesus' lordship," recognizing that Jesus is the Lord who rose from the tomb, which is necessary for salvation and the "subjective sense," which involves making Jesus Lord in a personal sense, which is part of discipleship.[11] It is possible under this view to be saved without ever making Christ the Lord of one's life. To maintain this it is necessary to argue that the title "Lord" when applied to Jesus means God rather than Master.[12] Another argument from this side is that it is obvious that Peter, and others, did not always make Him Lord (cf. Acts 10:14). The presence of exhortations to yield oneself to Christ as Lord is cited as evidence that it did not happen at the time of salvation.[13]

On the other side of the issue, it is maintained that people are to confess Jesus as God and Master. If He be God, how can He not be Master also? The confession in Romans 10 implies as much that Jesus is *my* Lord as that He is *the* Lord. There are several arguments given in support of this view. First are the demands of Jesus. One example is Jesus' command to the rich young ruler: "Sell all you have; give it to the poor; and come, follow me" (Luke 18:22). Following Jesus must of necessity mean leaving other pursuits and loyalties. Next, there is the call for repentance, by Jesus as well as the apostles (Matt. 4:17; Mark 8:34; Acts 2:38; 3:19; 4:32). John Stott argues that saving faith presupposes repentance. "Every man must to some extent . . . be concerned about his sins before he can be introduced to the Savior."[14] A third argument is that individuals must believe in Jesus, not about Him, in order to be saved. Faith must be directed toward Jesus, not just the facts about Him. It is also claimed that obedience and faith are synonyms. Hebrews 5:9 is cited, which says, "He became the author of eternal salvation unto all them that obey Him." Paul's apostleship was "for obedience to the faith" (Rom. 1:5). When people are freed from sin, they become a slave to Christ (6:14-22). The final argument is that in the Great Commission (Matt. 28:19) making persons disciples is equated with converting them to be Christians. In fact, it precedes baptism. There is no interim period between being saved and becoming a disciple.

The second view seems to be more in line with the New Testament as a whole, but some qualification is necessary. First, salvation is by grace alone, it is the gift of God. Not only is faith granted by God, but so is "repentance unto life" (Acts 11:18; see Eph. 2:8). There is no more merit in repentance than there is in faith. In addition, it must always be made clear that works are a result of faith and cannot bring about faith or salvation, but true faith certainly results in works (Eph. 2:10; Jas. 2:14-26). Finally, this is not to say that people ever become perfect disciples any more than they can have perfect faith, either at the beginning or at any other point in the Christian life. But, they can be a beginner or a mature disciple depending on the progress of their growth in Christ. Confessing that Jesus is Lord means not only that persons acknowledge that He is God, but that they intend to receive Him, however imperfectly, as Master. The answer to the question—Can individuals be saved without ever receiving Jesus as the Lord of their lives?—is *no!*

Binding and Loosing

One of the most controversial texts in the New Testament since the time of the Reformation has been Matthew 16:19, which says, "And I will give unto you the keys of the kingdom of heaven: and whatsoever you shall bind on earth shall be bound in heaven: and whatsoever you shall loose on earth shall be loosed in heaven." Upon this text a great deal of Roman Catholic theology on salvation is based; so it is important that we understand clearly what it means. The Catholic claim, based on this passage, is that Peter was hereby appointed pope with authority over the whole church and that some spiritual authority is passed on to his successors, the bishops of Rome. Therefore, all Christians must be in communion with the Roman Church, where Peter rules through his successors. To evaluate this claim, let us look at the text.

After Peter made his famous confession of faith that Jesus is the "Christ, the Son of the living God," Jesus said to him, "You are Peter, and upon this rock I will build my church; and the gates of hell shall not prevail against it" (16:18). Peter, of course, means "rock" or "stone." The Greek word is *petros*, which is masculine. It refers to a rock or boulder that may be thrown or easily moved. The term used in the phrase "this rock" is *petra*, which is feminine and refers to a mass of rock that cannot be moved. Some argue that in the Aramaic there is no separate term to indicate masculine. The word Aramaic word *kepha* would stand for both male and female. In this case it would be clear that Peter himself is the rock on which the church is built. However, as Lenski points out, "This appeal to the Aramaic substitutes something unknown and hypothetical for what is fully known and insured as true on the basis of the inspired Greek of the holy writers."[15] the Greek text does make a distinction between Peter and the rock on which the church is built. This is not a thoughtless change, but a play on words, which is meant to express something different.

For a moment, however, let us consider whether Peter is himself the rock of which Jesus spoke. (1) Even if he is preeminent among the apostles (and this is not certain), he is certainly not the universal head of the church. Ephesians 2:20 says the church is "built upon the foundation of the apostles and prophets" and Jesus Himself is "the chief cornerstone." Peter, James, and John are all called pillars of the church (Gal. 2:9). (2) The history of the church in Acts and the Epistles does not confirm Peter a place as pope. As Carr says (on Matt. 16:18 in the *Cambridge Bible*), "To history; Peter is not an infallible repository of truth." He was rebuked by Paul for Judaizing (Gal. 2:11), and it was James, not Peter, who presided over the church at the Council of Jerusalem (Acts 15). (3) The power of binding or loosing, if originally given to Peter, is expanded and given to all the apostles in Matthew 18:18. It is more likely that it was meant for all of them in Matthew 16:18-19 also. (4) Regarding Catholic claims, there is no evidence that Peter was the bishop of Rome. Traditionally, Peter was executed in Rome about the year A.D. 65. However, it appears that Paul preceded him in Rome (Acts 28:16ff.). Notice too that if Peter had an immediate successor in A.D. 65, the great apostle John who lived another thirty years would have been completely subject to him.

If Peter himself was not the "rock," on what is the church built? Another possibility is that the "rock" is Peter's confession of faith that immediately precedes Jesus' statement (v. 16). Concerning this view, Lenski makes an important observation: "The foundation of the church is not subjective but objective." "This rock" is not Peter's confession because the "church is not built on the confession her members make, which would change the effect into the cause."[16] If this observation is correct, then the rock is not Peter or his confession, but God's revelation of truth to him. Peter was only voicing the truth that had been revealed to him by the Father as stated in verse 17.[16]

Following this statement is the promise to the church that the "gates of hell shall not prevail against it." The Greek word translated "hell" in this instance is *hades*. *Hades* is comparable to the Old Testament word *Sheol*, which is the "place of the dead." The "gates" of a city was the place where the authorities sat in judgment. There are basically two interpretations of this phrase. The first emphasizes the idea of power or authority, and the powers of hell are Satan and his legions. The promise would mean then that Satan will never overcome the church.[17] The second view emphasizes the fact that *hades*, since it is the place of the dead, represents death. So then, the promise means that the church will never cease to exist. This writer must agree with John A. Broadus (*American Commentary* on Matthew): "Neither Hades nor Sheol ever denotes distinctively the place of torment . . . the gates of Hades (whether meaning entrance or power) cannot be distinctively the gates of the place of torment, the abode of Satan." If this be accepted, then the second view must prevail.

The phrase "the keys of the kingdom of heaven" may represent the keys committed to the royal household. With the keys goes some authority to open and shut. Isaiah 22:22 mentions the "key of the house of David" and the authority that goes with it, which was given to Eliakim. The authority that goes with the keys is also stated: "whatsoever thou shalt bind on earth shall be bound in heaven: and whatsoever thou shalt loose on earth shall be loosed in heaven." About this statement two questions must be answered: (1) To whom is this authority given? and (2) What is the extent of this authority to "bind" or "loose"?

As it has been previously discussed, some believe that this authority was given to Peter. If it were intended for Peter alone in this verse, it was not meant in an exclusive sense because the same authority is given to the Twelve in Matthew 18:18. A similar promise is given to all of the followers of Christ who were present after the resurrection in John 20:23. So it is concluded by many that anyone who preaches or teaches the gospel is using the keys to the kingdom. Calvin said, "Ministers of the gospel are like gatekeepers of the kingdom." They would "admit or deny admission, as they would forgive sins or retain them, by teaching the spiritual condition of admission or forgiveness, and by their inspired power of discerning and declaring a man's spiritual condition" (Broadus).

Concerning the authority to "bind" or "loose," the words themselves were common in rabbinical language to declare certain actions forbidden or permitted. The strict school of Shammai bound many things that the more liberal school of Hillel used. Some would limit the application of this passage to allow Peter to be the supreme rabbi with authority to forbid what is morally wrong or allow actions that are morally right. But it appears that there is much more at stake than moral questions. This statement "strictly denotes the forgiveness of sins" (Calvin). If it is not clear here, it is clear in John 20:23: "Whatsoever sins ye remit, they are remitted unto them; and whatsoever sins you retain, they are retained." Is then the power to forgive sins given to the church? It is necessary to look more clearly at the text to properly answer this question.

The *King James Version* and many others have translated the verbs "bind" and "loose" as though they are simple future verbs. But, they are perfect passive participles used together with the future of the verb "to be" (*eimi*) in the second instance of each verb and aorist subjunctives rather than future in the first instance of each verb. More exactly, it should be translated: "whatsoever you may bind on earth shall have been bound in heaven, and whatsoever you may loose shall have been loosed in heaven."[18] The same construction is also found in Matthew 18:18. What this means is vastly different from what it has been represented to say.[19] Only if the distinction in the tenses is ignored can one interpret this verse as meaning that whatever Peter or the church decides, God will endorse as correct. Conversely, it says that all that is proclaimed by the church must be based on the teachings of Christ. It shows how close the connection between what heaven says and what the church does should be, not the reverse. Harmony with Jesus' teachings is understood. The church does not dictate anything to heaven, but it operates under the direction of Christ, who is its head. Concerning this passage Broadus was correct when he said, "Ministers may teach the conditions of forgiveness, but they have no inspired power of discerning a person's spiritual condition, and their declarations of absolution are of no value beyond stating the conditions."

Wash Away Your Sins

In the account of Paul's conversion that he himself gave before the Jewish people at the temple in Jerusalem, Luke recorded one statement that has resulted in much debate: "Arise, and be baptized, and wash away thy sins, calling on the name of the Lord" (Acts 22:16). This statement has caused many to ask, is baptism the cause of our cleansing? Does baptism in any way effect our salvation? Many take a sacramental view of baptism and answer in the affirmative. For instance, J. R. Lumby in the *Cambridge Bible* comments, "Though the gift of the Spirit was announced, yet God directs that the means of grace, the sacrament of baptism, which the Apostle must offer to others, should also be received by himself." The well-known expositor R. C. H. Lenski adds,

> This is one of the cardinal passages on the saving power of baptism . . . What makes the present passage unmistakably clear is the second imperative. Why was it not enough to say, "Having arisen, let thyself be baptized, calling on his name"? Why was "and let thyself be washed as to thy sins" inserted if baptism and its water did not do this washing to remove the sins? The answer has yet to be given.[20]

There are several problems with the interpretation Lenski and others have proposed. In the first place, there are ten accounts of baptism recorded in the Book of Acts. In several of these accounts a clear statement is made about the relationship of regeneration and baptism. For example, Acts 8:12 says, "But when they believed Philip preaching the things concerning the kingdom of God, and the name of Jesus Christ, they were baptized." This indicates that faith is a requirement for salvation. While Peter was preaching to the Gentiles at Caesarea, the Holy Spirit came upon them; and Peter asked, "Can any man forbid water, that these should not be baptized, which have received the Holy Ghost as well as we?" (Acts 10:47). It is clear in this instance that regeneration has already taken place. In Acts 16:14-15 it says that Lydia's "heart" was "opened," and then she was baptized.

The most important passage in regard to the meaning of Acts 22:16, however, is Acts 9:18, which records another account of Paul's conversion experience. After Ananias had spoken to him, Luke said, "Immediately, there fell from his eyes as it had been scales: and he received sight forthwith, and arose, and was baptized." The exact moment of Paul's conversion can be debated, but one thing is clear. It took place sometime between his encounter with Jesus on the road to Damascus and the falling of the scales from his eyes. At whatever point it occurred, it was prior to his baptism.

The most serious problem connected with the idea of considering baptism to be a means by which God's grace is made effective is that it is contrary to the nature of grace itself. Ephesians 2:8-9: "For by grace are ye saved . . . not of works lest any man should boast." There can be no religious rite or good work required in addition to the grace (gift) of God, otherwise "grace is no more grace" (Rom. 11:6). On this subject Calvin commented:

> The question is asked, whether baptism is the cause of our cleansing. Certainly since the blood of Christ is the one and only expiation for sins, and since it was shed once for this purpose, and the Holy Spirit is cleansing us continually by the sprinkling of it through faith, the honor for this cannot be transferred to the symbol of water, without doing injury to Christ and the Holy Spirit.

However, some want to claim that baptism has some mystical connection with the receiving of salvation and the cleansing of sin. As Lenski put it, this represents "a real washing and not the mere picture of one." Yet, he does not want to deny that salvation is by "grace through faith."[21] However, one cannot have it both ways. Either baptism is necessary for salvation or it is not. If it is, then grace is in jeopardy.

Finally, the interpretation that favors baptismal regeneration runs into a third problem, the text itself. A literal interpretation reads like this: "And now what do you intend? Rising up be baptized and wash away your sins, calling upon his name?" There are two participles, *anastas* and *epikalesamenos* (rising up and calling upon), and there are two imperatives, *baptisai* and *apolousai.* Both of these are in the aorist tense and middle voice. Aorist would specify a once-for-all action, and the middle voice would convey the idea: "baptize yourself" or better "have yourself baptized," and "cleanse yourself" or "have yourself cleansed." Both of the participles mentioned are also in the aorist tense, which, again, refers to a once-for-all action. The time significance of these participles would necessitate that the action spoken of be prior to the time of the main verb in the sentence. So an expanded translation is, "After you have risen up, have yourself baptized, and have your sins washed away, having called upon his name" (author's translation). It is also possible to interpret the last half of the verse in this manner: "wash away your sins by calling upon his name." This is the proper translation if *epikalesamenos* is understood as an adverbial participle of means, which it in fact can be. If this is the correct translation, then it is clear that "calling on his name" effects salvation, not baptism. This is in accord with Romans 10:13, which says, "Whosoever shall call upon the name of the

Lord shall be saved."

Even if one rejects this interpretation, it has to be ad-mitted that since the participle is in the aorist tense, its action is prior to the verb. Therefore, the calling upon the Lord is the prior action. No one should deny that baptism is an important step of obedience to Christ for the new convert, but it cannot be the cause of salvation, although it is closely connected with it. One must agree with Robert-son that Luke was using "picturesque language" to de-scribe what takes place here, and he could make this state-ment because baptism is an outward reenactment of the inward spiritual change that has taken place.

So, in conclusion, one must reject the interpretation fa-voring baptismal regeneration in Acts 22:16 (1) because it would contradict other, clearer passages in Acts on the subject, (2) because of conflict with the doctrine of grace, and (3) because an exact translation of the Greek text does not require it.

Ye Must Be Born Again

The third chapter of John records what has become a very familiar story to us today, the encounter of Jesus with Nicodemus, who was a ruler among the Jews. Jesus' well-known statement to him was, "Except a man be born again, he cannot see the kingdom of God" (John 3:3). Lit-erally, the phrase "born again" means "born from above," "born a second time," or "born anew"; and all of these meanings are true about the new birth. The theolog-ical term for being born again is "regeneration." There is a Greek word that describes this event, although it occurs only two times and is somewhat rare in Greek literature as well. That word is *palingenesia*.

This term literally means a "new genesis" or "birth again." Kittell says that it may have reference either to a "return to existence," a "coming back from death to life," or a "renewal to a higher existence." In the Greek world, it was used primarily by the Stoics to describe the restoration of the earth after its destruction by fire, which they believed would come. However, it was not a new earth, but the old one restored to its former existence. In the latter part of the first century B.C., *palingenesia* was used to describe Cicero's return from exile and his restoration to rank and fortune. It is thus used in a more individual sense.

The word does not occur in the Old Testament, although a similar phrase is found in Job 14:14. It is used by the Jewish writer Philo to describe the renewal of the earth after the flood (*Vita Mos* 2:65).

In the New Testament *palingenesia* is used with both the cosmic and the individual senses. Matthew 19:28 speaks of cosmic regeneration. Jesus said, "Verily I say unto you, that you which have followed me, in the regeneration when the Son of Man shall sit in the throne of His glory, you also shall sit upon twelve thrones, judging the twelve tribes of Israel." The passage seems to refer to the times of restoration during the millennial period that follows the coming of Christ. The *Criswell Study Bible* says, "The key to that identification is the position accorded to the disciples of 'judging the twelve tribes of Israel.' Therefore, the prophecy must be millennial" (note on Matt. 19:28).

In Titus 3:5 *palingenesia* refers to personal regeneration. When people put their faith in Christ, they are born again. This new birth is the result of the mercy of God and the activity of the Holy Spirit. Works of righteousness play no part in it. The Holy Spirit "renews" them and makes them new creations. Thayer defines *palingenesia* as a "moral renovation," "the production of a new life consecrated to God, a radical change of mind for the better." It is a passing from spiritual death unto eternal life (1 John 3:14). Without it one "cannot see the kingdom of God" (John 3:3).

Chapter 5
Results of Salvation

A New Creation

The apostle Paul spoke of the conversion of a believer in Christ in the following manner: "Therefore if any man be in Christ, he is a new creature: old things are passed away; behold, all things are become new" (2 Cor. 5:17). The word for *creature* or *creation* is *ktisis*, which refers to the act of creation or the thing that was created. Another form of the word found in the New Testament is the verb *ktizo*, which originally meant to build or found. In classical Greek, it also assumed the meaning of colonize, or bring into being. The noun *ktisma* also denotes the results of creation.

In the Greek papyruses of the New Testament period, all three forms of the term are used. *Ktisis* (creation) is the regular term for the founding of a city (Moulton and Milligan). The noun *ktisma* (created thing) does not occur until this period. It is always used in a concrete sense. It is used to refer to the foundation of the world. The verb *ktizo* is is used to refer to the founding of a city, the establishment of friendship, or the creation by God of heaven and earth.

The verb *ktizo* is used sixty-six times in the Greek Old Testament. Of these, sixteen times it is used to translate the Hebrew *barah* (to create out of nothing). It is also used to express a variety of related terms. Its basic meaning is to express the "basic act of will behind the bringing into being, foundation or institution of something."[1]

In the New Testament *ktizo* and its cognate words occur thirty-eight times. The vast majority of these uses refer to the creation of the world as an act of God (Mark 13:19; Rev. 10:6) or of things that are part of that creation, such as meats (1 Tim. 4:3). Several passages, however, speak of the new creation, which is brought about through faith in Christ. Because of sin, people must be restored in order to fellowship with the creation. Even the inanimate creation "groans and travails" waiting for the restoration (Rom. 8:22, author's translation). The past, with the old person, is canceled out by the cross, and the new person is put on, like a clean garment. The nature of the new person is described in Colossians 3:10. It is "renewed in knowledge after the image of him that created him."

The purpose of this new creation is also described. Ephesians 2:10 says, "We are his workmanship created in Christ Jesus unto [for the purpose of] good works." (author's translation). God's purpose is fulfilled in this kind of obedient life. Our lives are to be an offering of thanksgiving, holy unto God. James said that God has begotten us "with the word of truth, so that we might be [infinitive of purpose] a kind of firstfruits of his creatures" (*ktisma*, Jas. 1:18).

Individually the believer is a "new creation," but not only that, he is part of a larger creation brought about by the cross. Christ has "abolished in His flesh the enmity" in order to make (*ktizo*) in Himself one new man out of two. The new man spoken of here is, of course, the church, which is created by bringing both Jew and Gentile together in Christ to make one new body (Eph. 2:15).

Finally, Paul made it clear that human works and ceremonies are powerless to save. He said, "For in Christ Jesus neither circumcision avails anything, nor uncircumcision, but a new creation" (*ktisis*, Gal. 6:15). There is no renewal without being "in Christ" (2 Cor. 5:17). Reformation of the old person is inadequate to save. The old person must be destroyed and a new one created. Human beings may make things, but only God can create. It is He who reforms the believers and makes them anew in the image of Christ (Col. 3:10). Faith, repentance, conversion, and regeneration would not be possible without the work of the Holy Spirit in the heart of persons. On the other hand, when individuals have received Christ and the Spirit of God has re-created them, it is just as impossible that the effects of that change never issue forth in good works.

Justified

The apostle Paul made a striking statement in 1 Corinthians 6:9: "Know ye not that the unrighteous shall not inherit the kingdom of God?" Examples of unrighteous behavior that he gave include sexual immorality, homosexuality, idolatry, various forms of thievery, and drunkenness. After declaring that some of the Corinthians had been guilty of these sins, he said, "But you are justified in the name of the Lord Jesus" (v. 11). Since the word "unrighteous" and "justified" are both from the same root in the Greek, Paul was saying the "unrighteous" are "made righteous." What did Paul mean when he said believers are justified?

The fundamental idea in righteousness is that of being in a "state or condition conformable to order." Involved in the idea of being "righteous" is the conception of a relationship, and it presupposes a norm by which to judge it (Cremer). The Greek word for *make righteous* or *justify* is *dikaois*. In classical literature to "justify" means (1) to deem what is right or fair, (2) to make something right, or (3) to do justice to someone. This may mean either to vindicate or acquit someone in the legal sense, or it may mean to judge (punish) the guilty. In the pagan world the standard of righteousness was set by social convention, which is in contrast to the biblical standard in which God Himself is the norm.

According to Colin Brown,[2] righteousness in the Old Testament is behavior that is in keeping with the two-way relationship between God and humankind. Therefore, the righteousness of God appears in His dealings with people, especially in His acts of redemption and salvation. In the Greek Old Testament *dikaioo* is almost always used in the legal sense. The rabbis generally identified righteousness with conformity to the law.

In the New Testament *dikaioo* is used to denote "justify" in the sense of "vindicate" or "show one to be righteous." In this sense wisdom is said to be "justified of her children" (Matt. 11:19; Luke 7:35). Sometimes it is used in this sense of people who try to justify themselves. In the introduction to the parable of the good Samaritan, a lawyer, "willing to justify himself, said to Jesus, And who is my neighbor?" (Luke 10:29).

Another more common New Testament use is to pronounce righteous and acceptable before God. In Paul's writings especially, God declares people righteous who put their faith in Christ. Through faith individuals may be acquitted of sin and pronounced and treated as righteous (Arndt). Romans 3:26 clearly states the point: "To declare, I say, at this time his righteousness; that He might be just, and the justifier of him which believes in Jesus" (see also v. 30; 4:5; Gal. 3:8). The theme of Romans is stated in 1:17: "The just shall live by faith." This is, of course, a quotation from Habakkuk 2:4, the interpretation of which was much discussed by the rabbis. The issue is, Does the verse mean "The righteous shall live by faith" (i.e., faithfulness to the law)? or, Does it mean "He who through faith is righteous shall live"? It is obvious that Paul took the second alternative, because the righteousness of God is not based on the works of the law (Rom. 4:5). Righteousness in the New Testament is firmly established in the character of God, not the works of human beings. He is the standard. It is this "of God" righteousness that is revealed by Paul in Romans (1:17), which is in contrast to the unrighteousness of people (v. 18). When people are justified by God, they are set free from sin (v. 18), made pure once more (1 Cor. 6:11), and are dead to the law (Rom. 7:6).

Some of the more important points concerning righteousness are these.

(1) Salvation is grounded in righteousness, which finds its expression in right behavior. In other words, if people are saved, they have been made righteous; and if they have been made righteous, then it should become evident by the way they live. Judicial righteousness (being declared righteous) should result in moral and ethical righteousness. As Peter said, Christ bore "our sins in his own body on the tree, that we, being dead to sins, should live unto righteousness" (1 Pet. 2:24).

(2) It must be emphasized again that righteousness takes its char-

acter from God Himself. It is not subjective, but objective in nature. It is not determined by the opinions of people or the whims of society. Righteousness is always in line with the character of God as He has revealed Himself in Scripture. In the final analysis, right living, or righteousness, is whatever God says that it is. It must also be added that because God is always the same, what is righteous or unrighteous does not change from one generation to another. Our perceptions and opinions may change, but real righteousness is constant.

(3) The Christian faith is called by Peter the "way of righteousness" (2 Pet. 2:21). It is the road of righteousness that leads to righteousness. We look for "new heavens and a new earth, wherein dwelleth righteousness" (3:13).

There has been a disagreement over the question of justification between Catholics and Protestants ever since the Reformation. "The Roman Catholic view set out at the Council of Trent regards justification as both an acquittal and a making righteous, and can even speak of an increase of justification . . . Scripture never speaks of justification by faith *alone*, and support for the ethical interpretation is found both in the Old Testament and in Jas."[3] Strictly speaking, the Catholic view is that God does not finally declare just those who are just until the end when they stand before His judgment seat, after they have been faithful to the end.

To come to this conclusion one must believe that there is a difference between real and imputed righteousness. But the truth is, imputed righteousness is the same as real righteousness. Believers are made the "righteousness of God in him" (2 Cor. 5:21). They are already a new creation. They do not have to wait until the judgment to be made righteous.

Many scholars have shared the view that *dikaioo* means

"to make righteous" because it is often used to translate
the Hebrew *hiphil*, which is causative in nature. God makes
believers righteous. One final question concerns the extent of this action. It obviously includes legal righteousness. Believers stand acquitted before God, no longer accountable for their sins (Rom 8:1). And not only this, they
actually receive the righteousness of God. Romans 5:1
says, "Being justified by faith, we have peace with God
through our Lord Jesus Christ." This is positional righteousness—that is God looks upon you as righteous because you are justified in Him. The rest of the believer's
life is the struggle with the help of the Spirit of God to
bring about moral and ethical righteousness in his life as a
believer. This part of our justification is not complete until God finishes His perfect work in us, when we meet Him
face-to-face.

Redeemed

One of the major themes describing our salvation in
Christ is that of redemption. There are three different
Greek verbs that denote the act of redemption. The first
of these is *exagorazo*, which in classical Greek means "buy
back," "buy from," "buy up," or "buy out of." It literally
means to "buy out of the market." The second word, *agorazo*, is the basis of the first one, and its meaning is "to buy
in the market." This word is especially common in deeds
of sale, such as in the purchase of houses; however, its
most noted use is to refer to the purchase of slaves. This
use is cited by Deissmann in a will dated around 133 B.C.
He expresses the opinion that Paul used the very formula
found in these records in the New Testament. The third
word is *lutroo*. This means "to redeem by paying a price."

It is commonly used in connection with redeeming articles that had been pawned, such as a cloak (Moulton and Milligan). It is also used in pagan religion to express the idea "freeing a soul from death." A different, but related use is to pay someone's expenses. *Lutroo* is also used by both Demosthenes (19.170) and Josephus (*Antiquities* 14.371) to refer to the freeing of prisoners by the paying of a ransom.

Exagorazo

In the New Testament *exagorazo* occurs only four times. It is a strengthened form of *agorazo*. It means to redeem by the payment of a price or "to recover from the power of another" (Thayer). It is used to describe how Jesus delivered us from the curse of the law (Gal. 3:13; 4:5) by being "made a curse for us," by being "hanged on a tree." In addition, *exagorazo* is used metaphorically in Colossians 4:5, which says, "Walk in wisdom toward those who are without, redeeming the time" (see also Eph. 5:16). The middle voice is used here, and the word for time is *kairos*, so the meaning is "to buy up every opportunity for oneself." Thayer adds, "Zeal and well doing are . . . the purchase money by which we make the time our own."

Agorazo

Agorazo, in the New Testament, means to frequent the marketplace or to buy in the market. In Revelation 5:9 it is used to describe salvation: "For thou wast slain, and hast redeemed us to God by thy blood out of every kindred, and tongue, and people, and nation." *Agorazo* is again used to describe the redemption of the 144,000 in Revelation 14:3-4. It is used many other times in the New Testament and is translated by the verb "buy." Paul said we are "bought with a price" (1 Cor. 6:20; 7:23). Peter accused the heretics of "denying the Lord that bought them" (2 Pet. 2:1). Whenever the price is described, it is always the blood of Christ, which was shed on the cross. (See also Mark 6:37 and Rev. 13:17 for other examples.)

Lutroo

The final word used in the New Testament for "redeem" is *lutroo* and its derivatives. It means to "liberate by the payment of a ransom." The noun form of the word, *lutrosis* is found several times in the Greek version of the Old Testament, the Septuagint. It is used in at least three different contexts. First, it is used to describe the redemption of property in the year of jubilee by the kinsman redeemer (Lev. 25:29). The redemption of those sold into slavery was described in the same passage (Lev. 25:48). Second, the redemption of the firstborn, which belonged to God, was also denoted by this same word (Num. 18:16). Finally, the redemption of a soul from sin is noted (Ps. 49:8; 130:7).

The verb *lutroo* is used in the New Testament with the natural sense of "delivering," such as "delivering" or setting the Jews free from the tyranny of the Romans (Luke 24:21). (See also Deut. 13:5 when Israel is redeemed from bondage in Egypt.) In the spiritual sense, it is used to refer to the work of Christ. Titus 2:14 speaks of Jesus Christ, "Who gave himself for us, that he might redeem us from all iniquity [lawlessness], and purify unto himself a peculiar people." This same idea is found in the Old Testament also. God desires to redeem a people for Himself and reveals it through David (2 Sam. 7:23). The price of redemption is further described in 1 Peter 1:18-19, which says, "You were not redeemed with corruptible things, as silver and gold . . . but with the precious blood of Christ, as of a lamb without blemish and without spot."

Another form of the noun *lutrosis*, *apolutrosis*, is also used ten times in the New Testament. It is simply a strengthened form of the word already described. It is also used to describe physical deliverance, such as from torture (Heb. 11:35). Like the other words of this family, it denotes spiritual deliverance as well. It is connected with justification and right standing before God in Romans 3:24. It is connected with "forgiveness of sin" in Colossians 1:14 and Ephesians 1:7. In both of these cases forgiveness is *not* without the shedding of the blood of Christ. Believers are redeemed from the sins under the first covenant by the death of Christ (Heb. 9:15). They are therefore set free to live a life of liberty in Christ (Rom. 6:14).

Not only is redemption spoken of as past and present, but it is also future. Believers are "sealed with that Holy Spirit . . . until the redemption of the purchased possession" (Eph. 1:13-14; see also 4:30). Again, the future redemption of our bodies is mentioned in Romans 8:23. Finally, *apolutrosis* describes the redemption of the people of God at the coming of Christ. Luke told us that when we see these things "begin to come to pass, then look up, and lift up your heads; for your redemption draweth nigh" (Luke 21:28). So then *apolutrosis* speaks of physical deliverance, deliverance from the guilt of sin, and deliverance from this world.

Several observations should be made after studying these various words for redemption. (1) The difference between *exagorazo* and *lutroo* should be noted. *Exagorazo* does not signify the actual redemption, but the price paid with a view to it. *Lutroo* signifies the actual deliverance, the setting at liberty (Vine). (2) Whenever any of these words denote redemption in a spiritual sense, they are never used in the active unless God is the subject. When people are the subject, the words are passive. In other words, people do not redeem themselves; God redeems—for Himself. (3) The paying of a price is mentioned over and over again; yet, it is not said to whom the price is paid. It is clear, however, that the price is paid in order to satisfy the righteous and just nature of God Himself (Rom. 3:26).

Sanctified

The apostle Paul in speaking to the Corinthians about their relationship to God made a very interesting statement: "And such were some of you" (speaking of their past lives in the world), "but you were washed, but you were sanctified [aorist tense], but you were justified in the name of the Lord Jesus Christ, and by the Spirit of our God." (1 Cor. 6:11). This is interesting because of the inclusion of sanctification with justification, and with both of them put in the aorist tense, which indicates a once-for-all action. Sanctification is often thought of as an ongoing process, but here it is presented as something God does at the moment of salvation. So, what does it mean to be sanctified?

The word Paul used is *hagiazo* (I sanctify). Other important forms of the word are the adjective *hagios* (holy) and the noun *hagiasmos* (holiness, sanctification). The verb form (*hagiazo*) is extremely rare outside the New Testament. In secular literature of New Testament times clear evidence of its use appears to be lacking entirely (Moulton and Milligan). Variant forms of the word (*hagizo* and *hagismos*) were appropriated in Jewish circles to denote their special concept of holiness. The letter *a* was added to the stem of the original word. The function of the word was unchanged, but it thus avoided association with pagan ideas. The pagan word means "to set apart for the gods" just as the Christian word means "to set apart for God"; however, "the set-apartness of the Greek worshiper was in character licentious, totally depraved, and sinful" (Wuest). In contrast, the biblical idea of sanctification incorporates the concept of moral purity. To be morally impure totally contradicts the nature of biblical sanctification.

The idea of holiness is very important in the Old Testament. God is called "this holy Lord God" by the Philistines (1 Sam. 6:20). The Messiah is called the "Holy One of Israel" (Isa. 43:14). Places are called holy. God spoke to Moses from the burning bush and told him that the place where he stood was "holy ground" (Ex. 3:5). At Jericho the captain of the Lord's host told Joshua to take off his shoes because the place where he was standing was holy (Josh. 5:15). People are sometimes called holy. The Shunammite woman said concerning Elisha, "I perceive that this is a holy man of God, who passes by us continually" (2 Kings 4:9). The Lord said to Jeremiah, "Before you came forth out of the womb I sanctified you, and I ordained you a prophet unto the nations" (Jer. 1:5). Not only are individuals holy or "set apart for God" in the Old Testament, but the whole nation of Israel was set apart. In Deuteronomy 7:6 we read, "For you are a holy people unto the Lord your God; the Lord your God has chosen you to be a special people unto Himself."

In addition, things which are dedicated to God are called holy or sacred. Also included is everything that is related to the worship of God. The city of Jerusalem is called the holy city (Isa. 48:2). David called the show bread on the altar "hallowed bread" (1 Sam. 21:4).

The verb *sanctify* is used to refer to purification from uncleanness (2 Sam. 11:4), especially when preparing to go into the presence of God (Ex. 19:10). On the other hand, holiness in the Old Testament is more than ritualistic cleanliness, it is moral and spiritual as well. The holiness of God confronted Isaiah with his own sinfulness (Isa. 6:3-7).

The New Testament uses the words denoting holiness in many of the same ways they are found in the Old Testament. (1) It is used to describe God—He is holy or worthy of reverence. The Model Prayer includes the phrase, "Hallowed [*hagiastheto*] be thy name" (Matt. 6:9). In the same prayer (Model Prayer) Jesus addressed the Father as "Holy Father" (John 17:11). (2) *Hagios* also is used to refer to "things which on account of some connection with God possess a certain distinction and claim to reverence"; these things are sacred and not to be profaned (Thayer), such as the temple (Matt. 24:15), Jerusalem (Matt. 4:5), the covenant (Luke 1:72), and the Scriptures (Rom. 1:2). (3) The most important use of the concept of sanctification in the New Testament is in reference to those persons who are set apart exclusively for God, such as the apostles (Eph. 3:5), the prophets (Acts 3:21), and the angels (Mark 8:38).

In addition to these special groups, the New Testament applies these words to all believers. Paul said that the "called" are "called to be saints" (Rom. 1:7). First Corinthians is addressed to those who are "sanctified [perfect participle] in Christ Jesus." This sanctification is described as something that has been completed at a point in the past with the results continuing until the present. The perfect passive participle is also used to describe believers in Acts 20:32; 26:18; and Romans 15:16. Not only does this indicate that sanctification is a state of being that is a result of salvation, but the fact that it is continually used in the passive shows that it is something that God does for the believer at the time of conversion. He sets the believer apart for Himself. This is called by some "positional sanctification." This one act of sanctification is made possible through the cross. Hebrews uses the aorist tense also when it says, "Jesus, also, that he might sanctify the people with his own blood, suffered without the gate" (13:12). Not only are believers sanctified individually, but collectively as well. Of the church, Paul said that Jesus gave Himself for it, "that he might sanctify [once and for all] and cleanse it with the washing of water by the word (Eph. 5:26). The idea that sanctification is an act that occurs at the moment of salvation is the dominant use of the word in the New Testament, so much so that believers are called "saints," even when they do not always act like it (1 Cor. 1:2).

On the other hand, the idea that sanctification is an ongoing experience in the life of the believer is present also. Peter said, "Sanctify the Lord God in your hearts" (1 Pet. 3:15). Hebrews 10:14 says, "For by one offering he has perfected for ever them that are being sanctified." Paul prayed for the Thessalonians that God might sanctify them "wholly" (1 Thess. 5:23). Christians are often commanded to be holy in life and conduct for they serve a God who is holy. The whole of the Christian life is the struggle, with the Holy Spirit's help, to bring our lives into conformity, actually, with the position God has given us positionally—that is sanctification. Paul urged the Corinthians to flee immorality on the basis of their sanctification (1 Cor. 6:11) and the indwelling of the *Holy* Spirit (v. 19).

The fundamental idea in holiness is separation from sin and for God. That means consecration of life and devotion to the service of God (Trench). The source of holiness is "the perfect purity of God which in and for itself

demption God has created a "peculiar people," a people
for His own private possession (1 Pet. 2:9).

Reconciled

To be reconciled is to be restored to a relationship of
unity, harmony, and agreement. According to the Bible,
people need reconciliation because their sin has caused
them to be alienated from God. God has provided the
means of reconciliation through the death of Jesus. The
Bible speaks only of our need to be reconciled to God, not
God's need to be reconciled to us. Although this is true,
the Bible is clear that reconciliation can take place because
Jesus Christ made atonement for sin through His death on
the cross. Thereby the holiness of God is satisfied by the
removal of sin, and the righteous nature of God is satisfied
by the great punishment of sin.

Katallasso

In the New Testament *katallasso* is used once in the context of the relationship of husband and wife. First Corinthians 7:11 says, "But and if she depart, let her remain
unmarried, or be *reconciled* to her husband" (author's italics). "Let her be *reconciled*" indicates that reconciliation is
something that must be acted upon by the estranged person; it is not merely something that happens to her. She
must change her attitude toward her husband. In this passage, the attitude of the husband is not described; however, it seems that the way is open for her to return to him.
But whether or not there is ill will on his part, she is still
commanded to be reconciled (remove the attitude of hostility) to her husband.

The most important usage, however, is in the context of the relationship of God and persons. Only Paul used *katallasso* in this way. The verb form is found five times (Rom. 5:10—twice; 2 Cor. 5:18-20) in this regard, and the noun four times (Rom. 5:11; 11:15; and 2 Cor. 5:18-19).

The primary emphasis of the word is on the change of the relationship between God and humanity, and, since God does not need to be reconciled to us because He is not our enemy, the change is a change that takes place only in us. Romans 5:10 speaks of reconciliation as taking place "when *we* were enemies" (author's italics). This change that is effected in those who believe is different from what is described by the word *justification*. Justification speaks of the removal of guilt in regard to the law of God and the restoration of our legal standing before God. Reconciliation goes far beyond that. Our whole life is changed. The statement, "If any man be in Christ, he is a new creature: old things are passed away; behold, all things are become new" is used in connection with reconciliation (2 Cor. 5:17).

A second point concerning reconciliation that should be emphasized is the fact that it is made possible only through the death of Christ. Paul said, "And all things are of God, who hath reconciled us to himself by Jesus Christ, . . . To wit, that God was in Christ, reconciling the world unto himself" (vv. 18-19). The emphasis here is not on the nature of the Trinity, but on what Christ has done. If God does not "impute" to us our trespasses because of the provision made in Christ, that is, His wrath is removed, does that mean there has been a change in God's attitude also? Certainly not. God always acts "according to His unchanging righteousness and lovingkindness." It should be noted also that anger, "where there is no personal element is a sign of moral health if, and if only, it is accompanied with grief" (Vine). Real love can exist along with righteous indignation, but love and enmity contradict one another. A perfect example of this is Jesus' attitude toward the Jews when they did not want Him to heal the man with the withered hand because it was the sabbath day.

Mark 3:5 records, "And when he had looked round about on them with anger, being grieved for the hardness of their hearts, he saith unto the man, Stretch forth thine hand." While God may be angered and grieved because of our sin, it is the result of His holiness that stands in such stark contrast to our sinfulness. However this in no way cancels the love of God that reaches out to humankind even "while we were yet sinners" (Rom 5:8). God always acts toward us out of love, not out of hostility. This should be made obvious by the fact Jesus died "for" our sins: "For he hath made him to be sin for us, who knew no sin; that we might be made the righteousness of God in him" (2 Cor. 5:21).

Another question that should be asked is whether persons are active or passive in reconciliation. Do people reconcile themselves to God, or does God reconcile them to Himself? The answer is both, or as it has been said, "The true answer is that they are made active" (Kittel). First, God has "reconciled us to himself by Christ Jesus." Then He has committed to us the "word of reconciliation" or the "ministry of reconciliation." And, finally, sinners are commanded to "be reconciled to God" (2 Cor. 5:18-20). God makes reconciliation possible, but individuals must act upon the offer God makes. God gives persons "both the right and the power to reconcile themselves to God" (Kittel). God does not force it upon people but entreats them to act upon His gracious offer. As it has been pointed out, if the wife who is told to be reconciled to her husband (1 Cor. 7:11) were totally passive, there could be no basis for fellowship with her husband. "Even if she is not to attempt reconciliation, she must at least agree to the attempt of the husband" (Kittel).

A final point that should not be overlooked is the scope of reconciliation. While it most certainly speaks to individuals and their relationship to God, it must be noted that the work of Christ was not for just a few but the entire world, and the invitation to be reconciled is not withheld from anyone. In fact, God has appointed ambassadors to beseech (plead with) people to receive His provision: "God was in Christ, reconciling the world unto himself, ... Now then we are ambassadors for Christ" (2 Cor. 5:19-20). In addition Paul said that the purpose of God's rejection of Israel was the "reconciling of the world" (Rom. 11:15).

Apokatallasso

Before this subject is completed it must be pointed out that there are two other words that are translated by the word *reconcile*. One is *apokatallasso*, which is exactly the same as the word mentioned above except for the addition of the prefix *apo* (from). In meaning it is exactly the same as *katallasso*. The preposition prefix only makes the force of the word stronger. It means to reconcile completely, to remove all enmity. It is found in Ephesians 2:16 when it speaks of both Jew and Gentile being reconciled with God. It is even explained that this means "having slain the enmity thereby." It is also described as the making of peace with God by means of the cross, the changing of a person who is an enemy of God into a friend of God (Col. 1:20-21). Since the word is not found in Greek literature before New Testament times, it is assumed by many that Paul coined the word.

Diallasso

The other word translated *reconcile* is *diallasso*. It is found only one time in the New Testament. It is different from the two words previously discussed in that it refers to the cessation of a mutual hostility in which both parties alter their attitude. In Matthew 5:24 it refers to the ending of enmity between two brothers rather than between an individual and God. Matthew said that if your brother has anything against you, "Leave there thy gift before the altar, and go thy way: first be reconciled to thy brother, and then come and offer thy gift."

A Down Payment

The apostle Paul said that believers are "sealed" with the Holy Spirit, which is the "earnest of our inheritance until the redemption of the purchased possession" (Eph. 1:14). The word translated "earnest" in the *King James Version* is *arrabon,* which denotes pledge or deposit of any sort. The word is probably of Phoenician origin and was introduced from that language into Greek. It originally referred to "earnest money deposited by the purchaser and forfeited if the purchase was not completed" (Vine). In classical times it was used in this manner to describe deposits required from public contractors to insure they would complete the job they started. It was generally used to denote a pledge of something else to come and, occasionally, it referred to a present or bribe. In the Greek Old Testament (Septuagint) it is used in Genesis 38:17-18,20, where Tamar requires a pledge from Judah (his signet ring, bracelets, and staff) that he will do what he promised.

In the Greek papyruses *arrabon* is used as a down payment on items such as cows or land. In a second-century B.C. note, a woman received a thousand drachma for a down payment on a cow. Receipts of money paid as a dowry for a wife have also been found. From ancient times till the modern Greek period, the engagement ring had been called the *arrabona*.

In the New Testament *arrabon* is used only three times. Besides Ephesians 1:14, it occurs in 2 Corinthians 1:22, "Who has also sealed us, and given the earnest of the Spirit in our hearts"; and 5:5, which also says that God has given us the "earnest of the Spirit." In these three passages several facts should be noted. First, God has given us part payment of the total obligation as a pledge that He is sincere. Paul said, "You were sealed with that Holy Spirit of promise, which is the earnest of our inheritance" (Eph. 1:13-14). God has given believers a guarantee that He will keep His promise, and the guarantee of our future inheritance is the Holy Spirit that all believers have received. The Holy Spirit is the down payment on what God has promised, and the down payment has never to be returned.

Next, Paul went on to say that the guarantee is good "until the redemption of the purchased possession." The purchased possession is the believer who has been purchased by the shed blood of Christ (Eph. 1:7). The promise to all saved persons is that their salvation is sure because it is guaranteed by the presence of the Holy Spirit who will remain until their redemption is complete. In addition, the *arrabon* is used in connection with the promise of a new, eternal body (tabernacle) with which we shall be clothed (2 Cor. 5:5). Paul said, "we know that if our earthly house of this tabernacle were dissolved, we have a building of God, a house not made with hands, eternal"

ly house of this tabernacle were dissolved, we have a building of God, a house not made with hands, eternal" (v. 1). He added that the One who has done this work is God, and He has given us the "pledge" of the Spirit that this new body awaits us. Finally, 2 Corinthians 1:22 adds that "the earnest of the Spirit" is "in our hearts." God has put His Spirit within those who believe as an inward witness to His ownership of them, which has the practical result of assuring believers that they belong, and always will, to God, and no one will ever be able to separate them from the love of Christ (Rom. 8:39).

Eternal Life

Three Greek words are translated *eternal* or *everlasting* in the *King James Version* of the English Bible.

Aion

The first is the word *aion*, which is translated *age*. Its primary meaning is "time, short or long, in its unbroken duration" (Trench). Sometimes it refers also to the world and all that exists in it during any certain time period. Often, however, it is used to signify eternity in several different ways. With the preposition *eis* and the article (unto the age), it means "for ever" (*e.g.* John 6:51; and Matt. 21:19). The phrase "unto the ages of ages" is often used to denote "forever and ever," as is the phrase "unto ages of ages" and other combinations of these words to refer to eternity. Jude was more specific when he said, "unto all the ages" (v. 25). On two occasions *aion* by itself means "eternal." In Ephesians 3:11 Paul used it to describe God's "eternal purpose" in Christ. Again, in 1 Timothy

1:17, Paul used *aion* to describe Christ: "Now to the King eternal, immortal, invisible, the only wise God."

Aidios

Another term, *aidios*, is used twice in the New Testament. Vine says *aidios* should always be translated "everlasting" rather than "eternal." *Aidios* excludes any thought of interruption and lays stress upon permanence and unchangeableness (Cremer). The instances where it is found are Romans 1:20, where it is used to describe God's "eternal power and Godhead," and Jude 6, where it refers to the angels who sinned and are therefore "reserved in everlasting chains under darkness, unto the judgment of the great day."

Aionios

The third and most common word for *eternal* is *aionios*, which occurs sixty-nine times in the New Testament. It refers to time without end or of unmeasured time. According to Cremer, it is used chiefly where something future is mentioned. Concerning *aionios* Moulton and Milligan say, "We must note that outside the New Testament, in the vernacular as in the classical Greek (see Grimm-Thayer), it never loses the sense of *perpetuus* . . . In general, the word depicts that of which the horizon is not in view, whether the horizon be at an infinite distance . . . or whether it lies on farther than the span of a Caesar's life."

W. E. Vine argues that there are three instances in the New Testament where *aionios* refers to a period of undefined duration, which is not endless. This is technically correct but somewhat misleading. The passages in question all refer to eternity, but a specific part of it, eternity past. The past, by definition, has an end: the present. Romans 16:25 makes reference to the "revelation of the mystery, which was kept secret *since the world began*" (literally the rendering is "from times everlasting"—author's italics.) Second Timothy 1:9 and Titus 1:2 refer to what God has purposed and promised "before the world began" (literally, "before times everlasting"). So every one of these references point to eternity, but only to that portion of eternity before the world began, which stretches into the past that is without beginning.

Not only does *aionios* refer to that which is without beginning, but that which is without end as well. In fact, everywhere else in the New Testament, it refers to that which is without end. In 2 Corinthians 4:18 it is contrasted with that which is "for a season." (See Philem. 15).

To see the ramifications of this word *aionios*, let us look at some of the persons and things that the word is to describe.

(1) There is God, who by His very nature is eternal. Paul said the gospel was made known by the "commandment of the everlasting God" (Rom. 16:26).

(2) Because they are part of the nature of God, certain characteristics of God are also described as eternal, such as His power (1 Tim. 6:16). The word *aidios* also describes God's "eternal power" in Romans 1:20.

(3) Another of God's characteristics is His glory. Peter said that God has "called us unto his eternal glory by Christ Jesus" (1 Pet. 5:10). (4) The Deity of the Holy Spirit is also attested to by the fact that He is said to be eternal. Hebrews 9:14 says that Christ "through the eternal Spirit offered Himself without spot to God."

(5) The future rule of Christ is said to be eternal. Peter said, "An entrance shall be ministered unto you abundantly into the everlasting kingdom of our Lord and Sav-

ior Jesus Christ" (2 Pet. 1:11). The angel prophesied the same truth to Mary, that He would "reign over the house of Jacob for ever" (*eis tous aionas*, Luke 1:33). If His kingdom is forever, then, of necessity, so is the King.

In addition to the above, several other things are said to be everlasting that relate to our salvation in Christ.

(6) The gospel is an everlasting gospel (Rev. 14:6). That implies that not only is there no other gospel now, but there never will be another, because the one we have will never be out of date.

(7) Redemption is spoken of as an eternal redemption (Heb. 9:12). This is in stark contrast to sacrifices of the Old Testament that were limited in their efficacy and temporary in their application. It is in contrast to the redemption proclaimed by certain of the mystery religions, which was temporary in nature. One rite called the taurobolium was supposed to give its participants immortality for twenty years (which itself is a contradiction in terms). In this rite the initiate was put in a pit covered by some kind of grate. Over him was sacrificed a bull, whose blood spilled down upon the candidate and gave him life (for a limited time). In Christ redemption is permanent.

(8) If redemption is eternal, then the salvation effected by it is also eternal. Hebrews 5:9 says, "He became the author of eternal salvation unto all them that obey him."

(9) Those who are saved are said to have "everlasting life" or "eternal life" (John 3:16,36; Matt. 25:46; Acts 13:46,48; Rom. 2:7; 5:21). Some attempt to argue that "eternal life" refers to a quality of life rather than to its duration. While there may be some merit to their arguments, the force of the word demands that the emphasis be placed on the fact that it is a life that lasts forever, without any interruption. This would preclude the fact that once people possess it, they can never lose it (die) or it

would not be eternal life. The Scripture says as much in
John 10:28, "And I give unto them eternal life, and they
shall *never* perish" (author's italics).

(10) With eternal life comes the promise of an eternal
inheritance. Under the new covenant, those who are
called will "receive the promise of eternal inheritance"
(Heb. 9:15).

(11) Along with this inheritance, the believer will receive a resurrection body that Paul described as "a building of God," one which is "eternal in the heavens" (2 Cor.
5:1). Paul also described this new body as immortal (1
Cor. 15:53) and incorruptible (vv. 42,54).

(12) Finally, believers will dwell in an everlasting abode.
At the end of the parable of the unjust steward, Jesus says
that the children of light will be received by God into "everlasting habitations" (Luke 16:9).

On the other hand, there are also several negative
things that are referred to as everlasting.

(1) The sin of blasphemy against the Holy Spirit is described as unpardonable. Jesus said that the person who
commits this "has not forgiveness forever" (unto the age),
but they are in danger of being in a state of "eternal sin"
(Mark 3:29, author's translation).

(2) The judgment of God is described as "eternal judgment" (Heb. 6:2). It is one, once pronounced, for which
there is no appeal.

(3) The fires of hell are described as "everlasting"
(Matt. 18:8). Those who are condemned enter into this
everlasting fire, although it was originally prepared for Satan (25:41).

(4) This punishment does not end. It continues for the
same duration as "eternal life." The same word, *aionion*
(everlasting), describes both punishment and life. Verse
46 says, "And these shall go away into everlasting punish-

ment; but the righteous into life eternal" (see 2 Thess. 1:9). Since this punishment never ends, it is not temporary but final. Its purpose, therefore, cannot be remedial, but punitive in nature.

The only conclusion that can be made is that there is an obvious finality that attaches itself to the decision one makes in this life. To choose Jesus Christ results in eternal blessing that begins now and never ends, and to reject Him results in eternal condemnation, from which there is no escape and no end.

The Kingdom of God

The last question Jesus was asked by His disciples is found in Acts 1:6. They wanted to know this: "Will you at this time restore again the kingdom to Israel?" It is interesting that they asked such a question because Jesus had spoken to them about the kingdom during a period of forty days prior to His ascension (v. 4). It seems that after Jesus' intense instruction in preparation for His departure, the coming of Pentecost, and the beginning of the church, the disciples were still expecting the coming of a kingdom. What is the nature of this kingdom? The Greek word for *kingdom* is *basileia*. The first controversy over the word involves whether or not in the New Testament it means primarily the royal power, dominion, or rule of Christ, or whether it refers primarily to the realm or kingdom over which Christ reigns. Moulton and Milligan believe that the root meaning of the word is the abstract idea of rule; however, it is easy to see the passage of the term into a more concrete meaning, the "line of our dominion" or realm. Both of these meanings can be illustrated in literature that still exists from the second century before

Christ. In the Greek Old Testament there are also several references to show that *baseliea* had already begun to refer to a realm, a territory ruled over by a king. For example, Psalm 135:11 speaks of "Og, king of Bashan, and all kingdoms of Canaan" (see also Dan. 7:24; and Ps. 68:32). In the New Testament there are many examples of both uses of the term. For example, during the temptations in the wilderness, Satan took Jesus and showed Him "all the kingdoms of the world" (Matt. 4:8). In the summary of the great heroes of faith the writer of Hebrews described them as those "Who through faith subdued kingdoms" (11:33). Jesus said, "Nation shall rise against nation, and kingdom against kingdom" (Mark 13:8). Herod told Salome that he would give her anything she desired up to "half of my kingdom" (6:23). All of these references certainly refer to physical territories or realms. On the other hand, *baseliea* may also denote a sphere of authority or rule rather than a physical realm. Paul said that Christ has "delivered us from the power of darkness, and has translated us into the kingdom of his dear Son" (Col. 1:13).

The vast majority of times when *basileia* is used in the New Testament, it is used in the phrases: "the kingdom of heaven" and "the kingdom of God." Some theologians want to argue that since *basileia* originally referred to "rule" rather than "realm," this proves that the kingdom of God is a spiritual kingdom where God rules, and, therefore, it does not include a millennial kingdom on this earth. However, it is clear that at least as early as 150 years before Christ, as well as in New Testament times, referred to physical realms at least as often as it did to spheres of influence. Since this is the case, one cannot safely argue that the kingdom of God is an entirely spiritual kingdom.

Another controversy that complicates the issue concerns whether or not the kingdom of heaven and the kingdom of God refer to the same kingdom. Thayer says "kingdom of heaven" refers to a kingdom that is of heavenly origin; it is "the rule of God, the theocracy viewed universally, not the Messianic kingdom." He adds that "the Jews were expecting a kingdom of the greatest felicity, which God through the Messiah would set up . . . over all the nations of the world. This kingdom was called the kingdom of God or the kingdom of the Messiah." Scofield also sees the two phrases as distinct from each other but does not agree with Thayer's view. In his note on Matthew 3:2 he says, "The kingdom of heaven (lit. of the heavens), is peculiar to Matthew and signifies the Messianic earth rule of Jesus Christ, the Son of David. It is called the kingdom of the heavens because it is the rule of the heavens over the earth (Matt. 6:10)." Again he says,

> The kingdom of God is to be distinguished from the kingdom of heaven . . . (1) the kingdom of God is universal, including all moral intelligences willingly subject to the will of God, whether angels, the Church, or saints of past or future dispensations (Luke 13:28,29; Heb. 12:22,23); while the kingdom of heaven is Messianic, mediatorial, and Davidic, and has for its object the establishment of the kingdom of God in the earth (*Scofield Reference Bible*, note on Matt. 6:33).

There is, however, a much simpler explanation for the occurrence of the two phrases: kingdom of God and kingdom of heaven.

The *Criswell Study Bible* says, " 'The kingdom of heaven' is a Semitic idiom in which 'heaven' is substituted for the divine name . . . This form of expression would appeal to Matthew's Jewish readers more than 'kingdom of God.' "[4] This conclusion that "kingdom of God" and "kingdom of heaven" can be used interchangeably is more plausible than separating them for two reasons. First, the phrase "kingdom of heaven" occurs only in the Gospel of Matthew. Matthew used it thirty-four times, while he used "kingdom of God" only four times. So it appears to be only Matthew's preferred terminology rather than a theological distinction. Second, when parallel passages in the Synoptic Gospels are compared, it appears that the two phrases are often interchanged. For example, after the temptation in the wilderness, Matthew said that Jesus began His ministry by preaching: "Repent; for the kingdom of heaven is at hand" (4:17). Mark, at the same juncture, said that Jesus began His ministry saying, "The kingdom of God is at hand: repent ye, and believe the gospel" (1:15). Similar comparisons may also be made in other cases (see Matt. 13:31; Mark 4:30; Matt. 13:33; and Luke 13:20).

The third controversy surrounding *basileia* concerns whether the kingdom it represents is present or future. Those who see *basileia* as primarily the reign of God rather than the realm over which He reigns tend to emphasize the present character of the kingdom of God. And there are passages that support the idea. Luke said, "The kingdom of God is in the midst of you" (17:21); Matthew added, "But if I cast out demons by the Spirit of God, then the kingdom of God is come unto you" (12:28).

However, the great majority of New Testament passages on this subject indicate that the kingdom is essentially future, although it is close at hand. John the Baptist began preaching that the kingdom was close at hand (Matt. 3:2); yet some time later when Jesus sent out the Twelve to preach, they were instructed to say that the kingdom was still "at hand" (10:7). In the Model Prayer, believers are instructed to pray: "Thy kingdom come" (6:10). Joseph of Arimathea is described as a man who "waited for the kingdom of God" (Mark 15:43). The disciples and others who followed Jesus as He approached Jerusalem for the last time before the cross were expecting that the kingdom of God would "immediately appear" (Luke 19:11), but the implication was that the time was not yet. Acts 1:6 also indicates that the time was not yet. The apostle Paul spoke of the kingdom as essentially future:

> "Know ye not that the unrighteous shall not inherit the kingdom of God?" (1 Cor. 6:9). "Of the which I tell you before, as I have also told you in time past, that they which do such things shall not inherit the kingdom of God" (Gal. 5:21); Flesh and blood cannot inherit the kingdom of God (1 Cor. 15:50)." "I charge thee therefore before God, and the Lord Jesus Christ, who shall judge the living and the dead at his appearing and his kingdom" (2 Tim. 4:1).

How then can the kingdom be both present and future? The answer is given very simply by Jesus in the parable of the mustard seed (Matt. 13:31-32; see Mark 4:30-32). The mustard seed is the smallest of all seeds, "but when it is grown, it is the greatest among herbs." The point of this comparison is the growth of the kingdom. Today it is with us in seed form, but someday it will be in full bloom. Today it is significant only to the believers, but then it will encompass the whole earth and all that are in it. As W. E. Vine puts it, "Thus at the present time and so far as the earth is concerned, where the King is and where His rule is acknowledged, is, first, in the heart of the individual believer, Acts 4:19; Eph. 3:17; 1 Pet. 3:15; and then in the churches of God, 1 Cor. 12:3,5,11; 14:37; cp. Col. 1:27." But even though the believers have been translated "into the kingdom of his dear Son" (Col. 1:13), they are still to pray for the kingdom in its fullness to come and they can understand the question of the early disciples in Acts 1:6, "Lord, will you at this time restore again the kingdom to Israel?"

Specific teachings about the kingdom may be divided into four categories. (1) Its beginning is described in the parable of the mustard seed (Matt. 13:31ff.). (2) Its progress is described in the parable of the wheat and tares (Matt. 13:24-30) and the parable of unconscious growth (Mark 4:26-29).(3) The conditions for entering the kingdom are described in several passages. Persons must become as little children (Matt. 18:3), they must have on the proper garments (22:12), they must be ready (25:1-13), they must be born again (John 3:3-5), and they must have been cleansed of sin (1 Cor. 6:9-11; Gal. 5:19-21). (4) Finally, the benefits of the kingdom are variously described. Those who enter will "shine forth as the sun" (Matt. 13:43), they will receive their inheritance there (Heb. 12:28; Matt. 5:5), they shall sit down with the saints of all ages (Matt. 8:11), and best of all, they shall be with Jesus, for it is His kingdom.

The Eternal Abode

One of the great promises of the Word of God is that believers go to heaven to be with the Lord Jesus when they die. This promise is voiced by the apostle Paul in 2 Corinthians 5:1, which says, "For we know that if our earthly house of this tabernacle were dissolved, we have a building of God, an house not made with hands, eternal in the heavens." In Hebrews 12:22-23, the Scripture identifies the "heavenly Jerusalem" as the city of the living God, the abode of angels, and the destination of the church, which is made up of all who believe in Jesus. Jesus Himself promised the disciples as much when He said, "In my Father's house are many mansions; . . . I go to prepare a place for you. And if I go and prepare a place for you, I will come again, and receive you unto myself" (John 14:2-3). The word that is used to denote our eternal abode, *heaven*, is the Greek word *ouranos*. In classical Greek literature *ouranos* was used to refer to: (1) the vault or firmament of heaven, including the sky and the stars in it; (2) the abode of the gods—it was sometimes called the portion of Zeus; (3) the space above the earth, the air; (4) later it was expanded to denote the astronomical heaven or the universe; (5) finally, it might refer to the place whose climate would cause one to call it "heaven."

In the New Testament *ouranos* is used in two basic ways. First, it is used to denote the "vaulted expanse of the sky with all the things visible in it" (Thayer). Some references are to the heavens, as opposed to the earth. Second Peter 3:10 demonstrates this distinction: "The heavens shall pass away with a great noise, and the elements shall melt with fervent heat, the earth also and the works that are therein shall be burned up." This includes the aerial heavens where the clouds gather. For example, *ouranos* is translated "sky" in Matthew 16:2. Also included are the regions of the stars. The phrase "the stars of the sky" (*ouranos*, Heb. 11:12) is an example of this use of the word.

The second basic use of *ouranos* in the New Testament is to refer to that eternal and perfect place where God Himself dwells. This heaven is invisible and spiritual in nature. It is what Moses calls "the heaven of heavens" (Deut. 10:14).

There has been considerable discussion about Paul's statement in 2 Corinthians 12:2 about being "caught up to the third heaven." In rabbinical teaching a belief in a hier-archical series of seven heavens is found (Testament of the Twelve Patriarchs, Levi 3:3), as well as in Zoroastrian thought. However, there is no evidence in Scripture to support such a view. One must agree with Irenaeus that being caught up to the third heaven would not be so great, if there were still four heavens beyond that (*Against Heresies* 2.30.7). It is more likely that Paul was thinking of the first heaven as atmosphere, the second as "comprized of the stellar universe," and the third "as the unique dwelling place of God"[5]

However, P. E. Hughes makes a very important point when he says:

> Despite the assurances of Rudolf Bultmann and many other modern writers, it is not a simple question of a naive, prescientific conception of a three-storied universe with which we are confronted in Scripture. The question is one of transcendence and preeminence, and this can only be expressed metaphorically by the use of 'local' terms such as 'above,' 'beyond,' 'higher,' and so on, just as in our so-called scientific age they are necessarily also used meta-phorically in everyday speech *and* in scientific language to express the ideas involved in graduation, comparison, and authority.[6]

As Westcott puts it, "Christ not merely ascended up to heaven in the language of space, but transcended the limi-tations of space"[7] (Commentary on Heb. 3:14). Hughes is correct also when he says that the presence of the plural form "heavens" in the New Testament is "probably due to the influence of the Hebrew term *shamayim* which is dual in form. The plural form is, in general, used inter-changeably with the singular in the New Testament,"[8] is also spoken of as God's throne (v. 34). God's voice is heard from heaven at the baptism of Jesus (Mark 1:11), and it is the place from which the Spirit is sent on the same occasion (Matt 3:16). God is so closely connected with heaven that heaven is sometimes used as a substitute for God. The prodigal, for instance, confessed to his father that he had sinned against heaven (Luke 15:18,21). In addition, God is the Creator of His own dwelling place, heaven (Acts 4:24; 14:15).

Heaven is also the dwelling place of angels (the messengers of God, Matt. 24:36), the abode of Christ, and the final home of believers in Christ. Concerning Christ several facts are mentioned in the New Testament. It is the place from which Christ came to earth. John said, "No man has ascended up to heaven, but he that came down from heaven, even the Son of man which is in heaven" (John 3:13). Heaven is the place to which Jesus ascended after His resurrection. He is now seated at the Father's right hand (Mark 14:62). Luke said that heaven must receive Him until the time of restoration (Acts 3:21). When that comes, it is from heaven that Jesus will return to earth. He will come in the clouds of heaven (Matt. 26:64). Paul said we are to "wait for His Son from heaven" (1 Thess. 1:10). Like the Father, Jesus is also spoken of as the Creator of heaven, earth, and all that is in them (Col. 1:16).

Concerning believers Scripture records several things. (1) Believers' names are "written in heaven" (Luke 10:20). (2) Their true citizenship is there (Phil. 3:20). (3) It is in heaven that a glorified body awaits believers. Paul said, "We groan, earnestly desiring to be clothed upon with our house which is from heaven" (2 Cor. 5:2). (4) Any reward believers shall receive for faithful service to God awaits in heaven. Jesus said that anyone who is persecuted for His sake should "rejoice, and be exceeding glad; for great is your reward in heaven" (Matt. 5:12). These rewards are also spoken of as "treasures in heaven" (Matt. 6:20). (5) The believers' inheritance awaits there. Peter said that we have an "inheritance incorruptible, and undefiled, and that fadeth not away, reserved in heaven" for us (1 Peter 1:4). (6) The believers' whole salvation and hope are bound up in heaven. Paul gave thanks for the "hope which is laid up for you in heaven" (Col. 1:5). In conclusion, it is clear that the destiny of believers is heaven; it is there they will live with Christ, serve and worship Him forever.

Chapter 6
The Assurance of Salvation

Fallen Away from Grace

In Galatians 5:4 there is a phrase that has become common in theological discussions. To describe a person who claims to have once had salvation and then lost it, the phrase "fallen from grace" is used. However, it seems that this use is totally foreign to the original context in which it first appeared. Just what did Paul mean by this phrase?

First of all, let us consider the context in which this phrase appears. It is used immediately after the allegory of Hagar and Sarah in chapter 4:21-31. Hagar is representative of the law and the bondage legalism brings. Sarah represents grace and the freedom it brings. Paul recalled the command God gave to Abraham in Genesis 21:10: "Cast out the bondwoman and her son, for the son of the bondwoman shall not be heir with the son of the freewoman" (Gal. 4:30). The admonition to the churches of Galatia based on this Old Testament passage is found in Galatians 5:1: "Stand fast in the liberty wherewith Christ has made us free, and be not entangled again with the yoke of bondage." The yoke of bondage, of course, is the law.

Paul then began to describe the consequences of attempting to attain righteousness by means of keeping the provisions of the law. One example is circumcision (5:2-3). If a person tries to save himself by works, then "Christ will profit him nothing" (v. 2); the death of Christ will no longer be effective for him (v. 4). As Lightfoot puts it, Ye are then and there shut out from Christ."[1] By that one act (aorist tense), you are placed in the category with Hagar, your mother, and therefore are to be driven out or banished from Christ.

The phrase "whoever of you are justified by the law" also needs some explanation. The verb "justified" (*dikaiousthe*) is in the present tense so it should carry the idea of a continuous action. Burton argues against this conclusion in favor of the view that it cannot be taken in the present tense (are justified) because Paul "thinks of justification not as a process but an act, and more decisively by his repeated assertion that no man is actually justified in law."[2] It is clear from Romans 3:20 and Galatians 3:11 that no one was ever justified by works. But still, Paul used the present tense for a reason. Though individuals cannot be saved by works, many are attempting to be justified in this manner, and all those who do so must continue to do so. The present signifies that it is a never-ending job. All who start out to follow the law can never stop or they will fail to reach their ultimate goal.

On the other hand, those who make this attempt, and there evidently were some among the Galatians who had made this choice, have already by their choice made the death of Christ of no effect for them and have "fallen out of grace" (aorist tense). "Grace" is preceded by a definite article and should be rendered "this grace." This grace refers specifically to the grace of God, which is the distinctive element in the gospel Paul preached. To "fall out of grace" is to separate oneself from the grace of God by the deliberate choice of the futile attempt to justify oneself by the keeping of the Mosaic law. These two approaches to salvation are mutually exclusive. "One cannot with intellectual consistency conceive of God as the bookkeeping God of legalism and at the same time the gracious God of the Pauline gospel, who accepts men because of their faith."[3] One cannot live keeping the statutes of the law and live a life of faith at the same time.

In conclusion, it should be clear to any student of the Scriptures that Galatians 5:4 has nothing to do with the losing of one's salvation. It has to do with rejection of the grace of God in favor of the law. Those who have made such a choice will demonstrate ultimately that they never experienced the grace of God in the first place. Those who want to argue that persons may lose their salvation will have to argue from some other point, because this teaching is not to be found in this text.

Adopted

Huiothesia (adoption) is formed by combining *huios* (son) and *thesis* (a placing) and literally means "the placing as a son" or "adoption." Vine says that *huiothesia* "signifies the place and condition of a son given to one to whom it does not naturally belong."

In the Greek world the word is found only as early as the second century B.C.; however, the concept of adoption (place a son) is much earlier. In Crete (fifth century B.C.) adoption had "to take place on the market-square before the assembled citizens and from the speaker's tribunal.

The rules allowed adoption even when there were already male descendants . . . The adopted son is introduced . . . and inscribed in the *koina grammateia.*"[4] This process was usually connected with the making of a will. Moulton and Milligan cite an example from the Greek papyruses:

> We agree, Heracles and his wife Isarion on the one part, that we have given away to you, Horion, for adoption our son Patermouthis, aged about two years, and I Horion on the other part, that I have him as my own son so that the rights proceeding from succession to my inheritance shall be maintained for him.

In the Jewish world official adoption was not practiced. The word is not used at all in the Old Testament. It is referred to by Jews living outside Israel, such as Philo. However, he used it in a figurative sense to refer to the relation of the wise person to God.

In Roman society the father had absolute power over his family; in the early days, at least, he had power of life and death over them. Barclay adds, "In regard to his father a Roman son never came of age. No matter how old he was, he was still under the *patria potestas.*"[5] Therefore, for a son to be adopted, he had to be transferred from under the authority of his father to another's, which was equally absolute. There were two steps. The first step was called *mancipatio.* It consisted of a mock sale in which the father twice symbolically sold his son, and twice bought him back. The third time he did not buy him back. The second step was a ceremony called *vindicatio.* The new father went to a Roman magistrate and presented the proposed adoption before him. When this was finished, the adoption was complete. This ceremony was carried out in the presence of seven witnesses. This was in case some dispute arose after the death of the adopting father, so that the inheritance of the adopted person was guaranteed.

In the New Testament "adoption" is used only by Paul. On one occasion he referred to Israel's adoption by God as His chosen people (Rom. 9:4). The other four references speak of the believer's relationship with God. Romans 8:15 says, "For you have not received the spirit of bondage again to fear; but you have received the Spirit of adoption, whereby we cry, Abba, Father." In the same chapter (v. 23), adoption is spoken of as future (at least partially): "But ourselves also, which have the firstfruits of the Spirit, even we ourselves groan within ourselves, waiting for the adoption, the redemption of our body." Galatians 4:5 gives further explanation of this concept of adoption. Jesus came to redeem those under the law "that we might receive the adoption of sons." Then Paul spoke of adoption as already complete: "And because you *are* sons, God has sent forth the Spirit of His Son into your hearts" (author's italics). Ephesians 1:5 explains that adoption was part of God's will from ages past: "Having predestinated us unto the adoption of children by Jesus Christ to himself according to the good pleasure of His will."

The use of *huiothesia* in the New Testament can be summarized as follows. First, it speaks of the special relationship believers have with God. It speaks of "sonship," but one distinct from that assured by natural descent. In this respect the believers are contrasted with Jesus. Believers are put into the relationship of sons by adoption; Jesus is the unoriginated, unique Son who always was the Son and therefore did not need to be adopted. Second, it is the Holy Spirit who is the Spirit of adoption who is given to us as a permanent witness to our adoption. It is the Spirit who assures believers of their relationship with God and causes them to cry "Abba, Father" (Rom. 8:15; Gal. 4:5). And not only this, but it is the Spirit who assures believers of their freedom from the bondage of the law (Gal. 4:5) and frees them from fear (Rom. 8:15). Finally, while adoption is a present possession for believers, it also has a future aspect. Although believers have received the "firstfruits of the Spirit," they are still waiting for the redemption of the body, which is considered to be part of "the adoption" (Rom. 8:23). It will be complete only when Jesus returns and changes this vile body into a glorified one.

Adoption, as it was practiced in the Roman world of Paul's day, meant three things. Barclay points out, "The adopted person lost all rights in his old family, and gained all the rights of a fully legitimate son in his new family. In the most literal sense, and in the most binding legal way, he got a new father."[6] Next, he became an heir to his new father's estate. No matter how many other sons there were at the time or how many were born thereafter, he was co-heir with them. This was not subject to change.

Finally, the old life of the adoptee was completely erased. All debts were legally canceled. He was regarded by the law as a new person. Barclay cites a case in Roman history that shows how completely this was true. The Roman emperor Claudius adopted Nero so that Nero could succeed him as emperor. Claudius had a daughter named Octavia. Nero wished to marry Octavia to seal the alliance. Although they were not blood relations, in the eyes of the law they were now brother and sister and could not marry. The Roman senate had to pass a special law in order for them to marry.

In like manner, believers, when they are adopted, are removed from under the authority of Satan and given a new Lord, who is now also their Father. They are guaranteed an inheritance with all the children of God, of which the Holy Spirit is the down payment and guarantee. The Spirit is also the witness that adoption has taken place. Finally, they are new persons, all their sins are forgiven, and they have a clean slate before God. What a tremendous blessing to know that God has made us His own.

Sealed with the Spirit

One of the most interesting words the apostle Paul used to describe the state of believers once they are "in Christ" is *sphragizo*, which means "to seal, to set a seal upon, or to mark with a seal." It is used fifteen times in the New Testament, eight of which are found in the Revelation. Three times Paul spoke of being "sealed" with the Holy Spirit. Ephesians 4:30 says, "Grieve not the Holy Spirit of God, whereby you are sealed unto the day of redemption." Again, Paul said, "Having believed, you were sealed with the Holy Spirit of promise, which is the earnest of our inheritance" (Eph. 1:13-14; see also 2 Cor. 1:22). What does it mean to be "sealed"?

In classical Greek *sphragizo* has four basic meanings (Liddell and Scott). (1) It means "to close or enclose with a seal." This sealing was to protect the contents of the thing sealed from theft or any kind of tampering. Liddell and Scott cite an instance where one is instructed to "seal up with his seal a sample (of the corn)." (2) It was used to authenticate a document with hot wax imprinted with a signet ring to guarantee the authenticity of the document in much the same manner that the seal of the notary is affixed to a document today to guarantee the authenticity of the signatures contained thereon. (3) It may refer to the certifying of an object after examination as genuine or as approval (see Herodotus 2:38). (4) Finally, an article may be sealed to show that it has been pledged. When the Roman general Cinna was captured by his enemies, he offered his signet ring to the centurion to spare him. But the man said, "I have not come to seal a surety, but to punish a lawless and wicked tyrant." (Plutarch *Pompey* 5)

In the Greek Old Testament *sphragizo* is used in Daniel 6:17 in reference to the sealing of the lion's den in order to guarantee that it could not be opened. In that case both parties affixed their seal so that neither could open it without the knowledge of the other. (See 1 Kings 21:8 for an example of its use in place of a signature.)

The Greek papyruses discovered from this period also shed some light on the background and meaning of *sphragizo*. Examples abound of sealing things for the sake of security, in order to protect the contents of the thing sealed. For instance, it was protection against falsification of a document. One third-century fragment says, "I gave the letter sealed (to the messenger) on the 12th together with the letters for you" (Moulton and Milligan). Another letter says, "I send you a box of very excellent grapes and a basket of excellent dates under seal." From the idea of security it is an easy step to the idea of "seal up" for the purpose of hiding or concealing something. Third, *sphragizo* also has the sense of distinguishing or marking an item to show ownership. A third-century note contains instructions to an agent to "send the donkey to be branded." Finally, the seal may also certify that an item was ready for delivery. Deissmann illustrates this meaning in a second-century papyrus written from one Chairemon to Apollonius, which says, "Seal the wheat and barley" conained in sacks, to guarantee the correctness of their acontents.

All of the four uses found in the secular documents are

also seen in the New Testament. First, when Paul said believers are "sealed with the Holy Spirit until the day of redemption," the intent is to guarantee that the soul is secure until that specified time. It means the same thing in Matthew 27:66. The Romans "made the sepulchre secure by sealing the stone." The object was to prevent its opening. The difference is that God is able to keep what He has sealed, sealed. Second, God makes believers and by this authenticates them as His heritage. Paul wrote, "It is God who establishes us; . . . he has put his seal upon us and given us his Spirit" (2 Cor. 1:21-22, RSV). He has put His mark of ownership upon us (See Rev. 7:3ff.). *Sphragizo* may sometimes have the connotation of sealing for the purpose of concealing the contents of something. The seven-sealed books described in Revelation 5 are an example; their contents were hidden. John was instructed in Revelation 22:10 not to "seal up the words of this prophecy." These were to be published rather than hidden. Finally, the seal was to guarantee the genuineness of the articles sent. If believers are sealed (Eph. 1:13; 4:30; 2 Cor. 1:22), God is guaranteeing that they are genuinely saved persons. A papyrus found at Oxyrhynchus confirms this meaning. A woman is instructing a friend or relative in a letter: "If you come, take out six artabae of vegetable-seed, sealing it in the sacks in order that they may be ready." Milligan comments, "The sealing was the proof that everything was in order, ready for delivery." In like manner, Paul, speaking about the contribution for the poor at Jerusalem given by saints in Macedonia and Achaia, said that he "had seen to it that the gift entrusted to his care had been properly secured" for those to whom it was intended.

It is a great comfort and a tremendous assurance to know if individuals are in Christ, God has sealed them, which means God has put His stamp of ownership upon them, authenticated them as genuine children of God, and secured them against any effort Satan may make to break that seal; and God intends for the soul to be intact "until the day of redemption." How much more secure could Christians be?

Heirs

One of the great promises of God to believers is that "if you be Christ's, then are you Abraham's seed, and heirs according to the promise" (Gal. 3:29). What is involved in being an "heir" of God? The Greek word that is used in this verse is *kleronomos*. Originally it denoted one who obtained a lot or portion. In Homer, for instance, it referred to a fragment of stone or wood used as a lot. The portion allotted by this casting of lots was the inheritance. Originally, an inheritance referred to that which had been received from the past. However, in the New Testament especially, the emphasis is changed somewhat to include the future as well.

In the Old Testament there are two basic ways the concept is used. (1) Captives and captured booty were divided among the victors by lots. Psalm 22:18 predicts the fact that Jesus' clothes would be divided by lot. The captives of Israel were divided among their conquerors: "They have cast lots for my people" (Joel 3:3). (2) The Land of Promise is Jehovah's inheritance. Jeremiah said, "You defiled my land, and made my heritage an abomination" (2:7). David said to Saul, "For they have driven me out this day from abiding in the inheritance of the Lord" (1 Sam. 26:19). The Levite was given no portion in the Promised Land for "the Lord is his inheritance" (Deut. 10:9).

In the Greek papyruses of New Testament times the word *kleronomos* is used in its ordinary sense of "heir." An example from A.D. 125 says, "If I die with this will unchanged, I leave my daughter Ammonous heir." However, a very important point is that being an heir usually involved responsibilities. A Macedonian inscription says, "But if my heir neglect anything he shall pay to the treasurer a fine of 750 denarii." Concerning *kleronomos* Moulton and Milligan conclude, "In the inscriptions the one thing most often emphasized is the obligation of the *kleronomos* to fulfill certain conditions devolving upon him as an heir. When Paul insists that only those who fulfill the conditions of heirship are truly heirs, he is making use of a well-known principle." It is interesting to find also that it was not unheard of for persons to refuse an inheritance because they did not want to take on the responsibilities or fulfill the conditions associated with it. Another papyrus cited by Moulton and Milligan says, "As I have no intention of entering on his inheritance, I am obliged to send you notice, that you may give instructions about the next step to be taken, in order to free me from responsibility after his death."

In the New Testament *kleronomos* occurs fifteen times. In most, it is used in the ordinary sense of an "heir," one to whom property is to pass after the death of the owner. Three Gospels record the parable of the wicked husbandmen who killed the son and heir of the owner in order to seize his inheritance (Matt. 21:38; Mark 12:7; Luke 20:14). Galatians 4:1 describes a child who is an heir but is too young to manage his own affairs.

Primarily *kleronomos* is soteriological in its emphasis. Abraham was appointed an "heir of the world" through the "righteousness of faith" (Rom. 4:13). Because believers are now children of God, they have become "an heir of

of God through Christ" (Gal. 4:7). The inheritance is es-
chatalogical in nature and at the same time present in effect. In Romans 8:17 the emphasis is on the future glory
that will be a part of being an heir of God. In Ephesians
3:6 the Gentiles are already fellow-heirs, part of the same
body with the Jews (the church), and "partakers of His
promise in Christ by the gospel."

Just as in the secular world where heirs had to meet pre-
scribed conditions in order to inherit, there are conditions
that must be met before one qualifies as an heir of God.
Noah prepared the ark by faith and became an heir of
righteousness, which comes as a result of faith (Heb.
11:7). Abraham became "heir of the world" through the
"righteousness of faith" (Rom. 4:13-14). Paul explained
to the Galatians that the only way to become an heir of
God is through Christ (Gal. 4:7). The inheritance that
God has promised to those who believe is based on the
condition of faith, by which we become children of God
and are placed in Christ, by which also we receive now the
righteousness of Christ. Having been made righteous by
the grace of God, we are also made heirs "according to the
hope of eternal life" (Titus 3:7).

Chastening

One of the factors that God uses to assure believers
both of His love and the believers' security in Christ is a
curious one indeed. It is spoken of in Hebrews 12:6: "For
whom the Lord loves He chastens, and scourges every son
whom He receives." The writer goes on to say that every
son of God experiences the chastening hand of God.
What does this word "chasten" include?

The Greek word used in this passage is *paideuo*. In classical Greek the primary meaning of the word was "training or education." It included the entire education of a youth, including physical education as well. Although the word primarily refers to mental training, it sometimes implies correction and discipline, which are occasionally needed for the benefit of the student. *Paideuo* is also used to describe the training of a child for the practice of an art, such as music, which takes much time and discipline to master. God is trying to train His children for the art of Christian living, which also takes much time, correction, and discipline to bring about excellence in them.

In both the Apocrypha and the Greek Old Testament, the meaning of *paideuo* is modified somewhat. Since the position of the Old Testament is that a child's education includes loving discipline (Prov. 13:24; 22:15), *paideuo* is used in this connection, and it refers to God's punishment for sin as well (Lev. 26:18; Isa. 53:5). It is clear that the predominant meaning of *paideuo* in the Old Testament is "education or training through discipline" or "instruction by correction or chastening." Another example is found in Psalm 6:1, where David said, "O Lord, rebuke me not in thine anger, neither chasten me in thy hot displeasure." Concerning the Old Testament usage of the word, Trench says, "They felt and understood that all effectual instruction for the sinful children of men includes and implies chastening, or, as we are accustomed to say, out of a sense of the same truth, 'correction.' "

In the New Testament, the classical Greek meaning "educate" occurs in Acts 7:22 where it describes the education of Moses "in all the wisdom of the Egyptians" (see 22:3 also). The New Testament, however, generally follows the Old Testament usage of *paideuo*. (1) It is used to refer to the "nurture" of children, which means to train them by act and discipline (Eph. 6:4). (2) *Paideuo* is used with its more severe meaning in Luke 23:16,22. Here Pilate desired to chasten Jesus and let Him go. The chastisement spoken of here is the scourge, which was a severe beating with a whip that often resulted in death. (3) In addition, *paideuo* sometimes refers to God's providential dealings with His children, those who are believers in Jesus. Paul said that "we are chastened of the Lord, that we should not be condemned with the world" (1 Cor. 11:32). John also spoke of the discipline of the Lord in Revelation 3:19: "As many as I love, I rebuke and chasten." (4) Finally, the judgment of unbelievers is also described by *paideuo*. Hymenaeus and Alexander were "delivered to Satan" that they might "learn not to blaspheme" (1 Tim. 1:20).

The most prominent passage describing the biblical meaning of *paideuo* is Hebrews 12:5-11. Several points are made by the author of Hebrews concerning the chastening of the Lord. (1) Believers are told not to "despise" (think little of, make light of) the chastening of the Lord (v. 5). The second half of the verse associates this chastening with being "rebuked" (punished, convicted, or exposed) by the Lord. (2) The author then makes it clear that chastisement is a sign of God's love for believers. It does not spring from the wrath of God as some erroneously conclude, nor does it contradict the love of God. God chastens His children because He desires the best for them, even though His chastening may sometimes be very severe. Verse six says that He "scourges [whips, flogs] every son whom He receives." (3) Chastening is a sign of a legitimate child of God. There are no true children who escape God's discipline (v. 7). All true sons "have become" partakers of it (v. 8). (4) The author implies that the way in which a father chastens his children has a great deal to do with what kind of respect he gets from his children (v. 9). Since God's discipline is always fair (deserved) and even-handed, believers should submit their lives to Him. (5) God's discipline is for our benefit, to produce the fruit of holiness and righteousness in us (v. 10). Moreover, it is a spiritual exercise intended to strengthen the believers (v. 11). If believers are aware of what God is trying to do for them by this discipline, when they stray from the will of God this very knowledge will comfort and assure them that God loves them and that they belong to God.

Partakers of the Holy Spirit

One of the most debated passages in the New Testament is Hebrews 6:4-6: "For it is impossible for those who were once enlightened, and have tasted of the heavenly gift, and were made partakers of the Holy Ghost, And have tasted the good word of God, and the powers of the world to come. If they shall fall away, to renew them again to repentance; seeing they crucify to themselves the Son of God afresh, and put him to an open shame." This passage has been a famous battleground between Arminians and Calvinists, and there have been many proposed interpretations. To complicate matters, there are not one but three important questions involved. First, were those described ever saved or were they always unregenerate? Second, what is the nature of this falling away? And, finally, is the resultant state of condemnation final or is it revocable?

To answer the first question, the four participles which describe the past experience of those in question must be examined. The word for "enlightened" is *photisthentos*, which means those who have "become light" or "have been enlightened." Ephesians 5:14 seems to indicate that this is a work that happens in a person's life only because of his finding Christ. Next, they are said to have "tasted of the heavenly gift." Exactly what the writer intends by "the heavenly gift" is difficult to say. However, it almost certainly refers to the gift of salvation: either directly or indirectly. Delitzsch maintains that *geusamenous* (tasted) means "to have a thorough experience or enjoyment of the object." It is not a superficial tasting. Again, being a partaker "of the Holy Spirit" is descriptive of one who has received the Holy Spirit and become a member of the body of Christ. The word "tasted" then (*geusamenous*) occurs a second time. It refers to a real experience of feeding on "the good word of God," which is nourishment for the believer, and a real experience in which the "powers of the world to come" have been seen in operation. The believer is now part of the kingdom of God which waits for its final revelation. From this description it does not appear that those in question could be any other than believers in Christ, if the passage is taken literally. However, there are those who disagree with this interpretation. But before looking at some of the interpretations which have been proposed, let us look at the other questions mentioned above.

What is the nature of this "apostasy" or "falling away" described? Tertullian taught that if one committed gross sins of the flesh, it was impossible for him to be renewed to repentance (*On Modesty* 20). The Novatians applied this passage to anyone who had denied Christ and refused to receive them back into the church. Most interpreters, however, are agreed that this does not refer to some moral or spiritual lapse, but to a complete renunciation of Christ and of His gospel. Delitzsch describes it like this, "*Parapesein* . . . is (like the 'willfully sinning' of v. 26 . . .) intended to denote such apostasy as not only withdraws from the ethical influences of Christian truth, but renounces the truth itself." Many others liken this situation to the unpardonable sin of blaspheming the Holy Spirit. It is obviously not something accidentally committed, but an act of open, willful rebellion against God.

The third question is, can the person who has thus defected from Christ ever return? There are some who argue that it is impossible to renew to repentance persons who have fallen away only as long as they do not repent. This interpretation is based on the participles *anastaurountas* (crucify again) and *paradeigmatizontas* (put to shame openly) which are both in the present tense and therefore signify a continuing action. On the other hand, the great majority of scholars disagree. For one reason, the word impossible means impossible. If one rejects the sacrifice He offered, there is no other one forthcoming. In addition, it must be noted that the participle *parapesontas* (fall away) is in the aorist tense. This signifies that the fatal change has come over them once for all. The present participles which follow would be taken then to mean that once that step has been taken, they will continue from that time on to crucify and bring shame on Christ.

There is general agreement on the second and third questions, but much debate still continues on the first—is this a believer who has fallen from grace or not? Delitzsch insists that it is a believer who has decided to reject Christ. He declares that to say there is no sign of true regeneration of the heart and will of those described here is a "groundless assertion." He says Hebrews describes a person who "renounces the truth itself; so that what was once an inward and familiar possession, is now become something merely external and alien."

In a different light, Calvin says that while "God certainly bestows His Spirit of regeneration only on the elect," he does not see "any reason why He should not touch the reprobate with a taste of His grace, or illumine their minds with some glimmerings of His light, or affect them with some sense of His goodness, or to some extent engrave His Word in their hearts." In other words, he believes there is some knowledge in the lost man which later vanishes away because it does not take root or is choked; however, the man was never truly converted.

F. F. Bruce takes the position that those described in Hebrews 6:4-6 were professing Christians but were not converted. However, his explanation of the passage takes a different line of reasoning. He understands the verb "enlightened" to represent baptism—a sense which some second century writers gave to it. The "tasting of the heavenly gift may suggest the Eucharist," but it may also include all of the spiritual blessings "sacramentally sealed and signified in the Eucharist." Concerning the phrase "become partakers of the Holy Spirit," he argues that it is not the Holy Spirit Himself at issue here, but "His gifts or operations." Simon Magus is cited as an example of the tasting of the "good word of God and powers of the age to come." He realized how good it was and was amazed at the signs and wonders which accompanied it, but did not personally receive it.[6]

In this manner Bruce avoids the doctrine of falling from grace. However, his argument is weak, beginning with the first point. Just because a few second century writers equated "enlightenment" and baptism does not mean that the writer of Hebrews did. It is also difficult to accept the conclusion that the heavenly gift is the Lord's Supper. Though ingenious, his argument is not convincing.

Another attempt to explain this passage is made by Kenneth Wuest.[7] He sees this as referring to Jews who professed faith in Christ, who had gone along with the

Holy Spirit "in His pre-salvation work, had been brought unto the place of repentance, to the very threshold of salvation." They had left the sacrificial system to accept the message of the New Testament but were in danger of going back to the law. He says, "These words 'falling away,' can only refer to the one sin spoken of in this book. It could only be committed in the first century and by a Jew, or a Gentile proselyte to Judaism, and for the reason that conditions since A.D. 70 have been such as to make impossible the committing of that sin." If this be true the passage would not apply to anyone in this age.

While the aforementioned explanations are also interesting, none of them are quite satisfactory. We cannot agree that Hebrews is speaking of one who was truly saved and then rejected Christ. On the other hand, even though Calvin, Bruce, and Wuest defend the conclusion, their arguments, while possible, are not altogether convincing. Therefore, let us look at another alternative. There is the possibility that the author is intending only to describe a hypothetical situation. *If* a person were saved, then willfully rejected Christ, he could not be saved a second time. That is a fact of which one can be sure. The question is, has anyone, or could anyone, ever do that? The author does not state that anyone is guilty of that sin. There are several reasons for this interpretation. (1) If it were not for the theological debate involved, no one would ever have taken verses 4-5 to refer to anything less than a fully converted person. "Every prominent word used is found applied to believers in other parts of the New Testament (Griffith-Thomas). (2) The phrase "if they shall fall away" is conditional (although the verb form is a participle, it is best to take it in this sense). It is not a statement of fact but of possibility. Tyndale translated it in this manner before the Calvinist-Arminian controversy began. (3) The author changes from using the first person (us, we) to the third person (those, they) in verses 4-6. In verse 9 he returns to the first person, which indicates that he is not speaking about any of the Hebrews but about a hypothetical third party. In fact, he says, "Beloved, we are persuaded better things of you, and things that accompany salvation."

In addition to these indications in the text, other Scriptures indicate that those who depart do so because they never knew Christ. Jesus says to those who professed faith in Him but did not really believe, "I never knew you; depart from me, you that work iniquity" (Matt. 7:23). Speaking of those who were against Christ, John says, "They went out from us: but they were not of us; for if they had been of us,. . . they would have continued with us: but they went out that they might be made manifest that they were not all of us" (1 John 2:19). Perseverance seems to be one of the proofs of a true believer. Moreover, it is difficult to to believe that anyone who had ever "tasted the good gift" and had been made a partaker of the Holy Spirit would ever desire to deny Christ, because his own experience would prove to him that Jesus is indeed the Christ.

Saved to the Uttermost

The High Priesthood of Christ is compared with that of Aaron in Hebrews, chapter 7. Because He continues forever, in contrast to the Levitical priests, Jesus has an "unchangeable priesthood." Because of this He is able to "save them to the uttermost that come unto God by Him"(v. 25). The phrase "to the uttermost," which describes the extent of this salvation, occurs only twice in the New Testament. The phrase in Greek is *eis to panteles*, which literally means "unto the completely."

Panteles is the neuter form of the adjective *panteles*. In classical Greek it meant all-complete, perfect, or entire. It was used to describe a "perfect" wife. It could also denote an "all-accomplishing" or "all-achieving" action. In answer to questions, it meant "most certainly" (Liddell and Scott).

In the Greek papyruses of New Testament times, *panteles* has several uses as well. In a property transaction it is used to denote the finality of the transaction (Moulton and Milligan). It describes someone who is "utterly" distressed, another whose duties are "completely" accomplished, and another who is "entirely" blameless.

The only other occurrence of the phrase in the New Testament is found in Luke 13:11, where it describes the woman with an infirmity who could "in no wise" lift herself up. She was "absolutely" not able. In Hebrews 7:25, the passage in question, the phrase is translated "to the uttermost." Just what did the writer mean to imply by that? In several ancient versions of the Bible (the Latin Vulgate, the Syriac, and Coptic versions), *eis to panteles* is translated with a temporal significance—"forever," or "for all time." This is certainly in accordance with the context of the passage. The believer is saved forever because our High Priest "ever lives to make intercession" for him (Heb. 7:25). The way of access to God is always open through Him.

"To the uttermost" may be meant to describe the extent of our salvation in Christ. In contrast to the law, which "made nothing perfect" (7:19) and was weak and unprofitable (v. 18), the salvation which comes through the High Priest after the order of Melchizedek is complete and entire. He does not need to continually offer sacrifices as the Levitical priests did, because His one sacrifice was enough to save us fully (v. 27). Anyone who comes to

God through Jesus is saved "to the uttermost." He is fully and completely saved. There is nothing else which needs to be done.

The problem is, it is difficult to tell which emphasis the author intended to give because both are true and both can be found in the immediate context. It is possible that he meant to say that not only are believers completely saved, but they are permanently saved. One thing is sure, a salvation which is so complete and so permanent could not possibly be lost.

That You Might Know

The key word in the First Epistle of John is "know." The purpose of the book is stated in chapter 5, verse 13: "These things have I written unto you that believe on the name of the Son of God, that you may know that you have eternal life." In the Greek text, however, there are two different words for the concept "know." There is *ginosko*, which occurs twenty-three times in 1 John alone (2:3,4, 5,13,14,18,29; 3:1,6,16,19,20,24; 4:2,6,7,8,13,16; 5:2, 20),and *oida*, which is found thirteen times (2:11,20,21,29; 3:2,5,14,15; 5:13,15,18,19,20).

Originally, *ginosko* denoted the grasping and understanding of things by the mind which came to it primarily by way of the senses. In other words, it meant knowledge gained by experience. This also included the interpretation of the data received from the senses. Schmitz says that it meant "to notice, perceive, or recognize a thing, person, or situation through the senses, particularly the sight. (Seeing and *ginosko* are linked in Homer *Od.* 15, 532 and 24, 217)."[8] Other applications of *ginosko* include these: (1) "to distinguish" between persons, things, or experiences; (2) "to know" or be acquainted with something in a personal way; (3) to denote a relationship between persons, "to know" someone; (4) to discern situations as a result of analyzing the information received, to judge as in a court situation; (5) even philosophical speculation was often regarded as seeing something, to know by reflection, to perceive. This last use of *ginosko* is parallel to the primary use of *oida*.

In the New Testament *ginosko* is used in very similar ways. (1) It means to know or come to know. This may include things: to know a tree by its fruits (Matt. 12:33), to know something by something. In particular, it is used of becoming acquainted with God and Christ and the things pertaining to Them. John 17:3, for example, says, "And this is life eternal, that they might know thee the only true God, and Jesus Christ, whom thou hast sent." (See Phil. 3:10 also.)

(2) "Know" may also be used with the sense of "learn of" or "find out" about a given situation. Cleopas asks, "Are you only a stranger in Jerusalem, and have not known the things which are to come to pass there in these days?" (Luke 24:18; see 1 Thess. 3:5 also). (3) To know sometimes means to understand or comprehend something such as a parable. Jesus said to the disciples, "Know ye not this parable? and how then will you know all parables?" (Mark 4:13). (4) *Ginosko* is sometimes used with its original sense, "notice, feel, or realize." When the woman with an issue of blood touched Jesus, He perceived that virtue went out of Him (Luke 8:46). (5) Finally, following the Old Testament usage, know can be a reference to having sexual relations with someone (Gen. 4:1,17; Matt. 1:25).

Thayer makes this distinction between *ginosko* and *oida*. *Ginosko* denotes "a discriminating apprehension of external impressions, a knowledge grounded in personal experience." *Oida*, on the other hand, means "to have seen with the mind's eye." It represents a purely mental perception. Knowledge of a work of literature gained by reading such would be signified by *ginosko*. Jesus' insight into divine things is described by *oida* in John 5:32.

Further examination of the use of these terms gives us a better insight into the exact meaning of certain passages. For example, when confronted by one of the maids of the high priest, Peter began to curse and to swear, "I know not this man of whom you speak" (Mark 14:71). He uses *oida*, which is more emphatic in this instance than *ginosko* because it implies he not only had no relationship with Jesus, but that he knew nothing about Him at all. On the other hand, when Jesus says that He will say to some, "I never knew you; depart from me" (*ginosko*, Matt. 7:23). He is not saying that He is unaware that they exist or that He never met them, but that He never had a personal relationship with them. The same is true of Paul's statement in 2 Corinthians 5:21, that Jesus "knew no sin" (*ginosko*). This does not mean that He had no intellectual knowledge of sin, but that He had not experienced it personally.

Regarding the Jews, the Scripture is clear that they as a group not only knew the law and God's will intellectually, but they had personal experience with it (Acts 22:14; Rom. 2:18; 7:1). The arrogance of the Pharisees on this point is demonstrated in John 7:49, where the common people are described as those who have no personal experience with the law. Schmitz comments concerning this statement, "It contains the implication that the common people would not have gone after Jesus if they had really known and obeyed the law."[9]

In First John the use of the concept "know" is primarily used in reference to "knowing" that we know Christ personally or "knowing" that we have eternal life. *Ginosko* is used with the emphasis on the kind of knowledge that results from one's personal experience. We know that "we have known Him, if we keep His commandments" (2:3). Loving in deed rather than word only is one way that we can "know that we are of the truth" and gain assurance in our hearts (3:19). Similarly, loving one another is more evidence from our own experience on which we can reflect and come to the conclusion that we know Him (4:7). The inward testimony of the Spirit of God in one's life is further evidence that one can experience to help confirm the fact we are "in Him" (4:13).

Oida, in contrast, is generally used when the acceptance or understanding of doctrinal truths is concerned. For instance, it is the believer who really understands what truth is (2:20-21). "We know that, when he shall appear, we shall be like him" (3:2), not by experience, of course, but we know it because we trust in His promise. Other facts we know, not by experience, but because we have been taught, include these. "He was manifested to take away our sins; and in Him is no sin" (v. 5). "No murderer has eternal life abiding in Him" (v. 15). "Whosoever is born of God [does not continue in sin]" (5:18). "We are of God, and the whole world lies in wickedness" (v. 19). All of these beliefs are expressed with the use of *oida*.

Finally, in the last chapter, verse 20, both *oida* and *ginosko* occur in the same verse. "We know [*oida*, as a historical fact] that the Son of God is come, and has given us an understanding, that we may know [by personal experience] him that is true, and we are in him that is true, even in his Son Jesus Christ." We can know that we have eternal

life because of what we have learned of Christ from the
Scriptures and from our own personal relationship with
Him. This is why John wrote," that ye may know that ye
have eternal life" (v. 13).

Notes

Introduction
1. William Barclay, *New Testament Words* (Philadelphia: The Westminster Press, 1974), 269-270.

Chapter 1
1. James Denney, *Expositor's Greek Testament: Romans.*

Chapter 2
1. William Ramsay, *The Bearing of Recent Discovery on the Trustworthiness of the New Testament.*
2. See Deissmann, *Light from the Ancient East* (New York: George H. Doran, 1927); Moulton and Milligan.
3. Colin Brown, ed. *Dictionary of New Testament Theology,* 3 vols. (Grand Rapids: Zondervan Publishing House, 1976).
4. Ibid.
5. Kenneth S. Wuest. *Wuest's Word Studies.* 4 vols. (Grand Rapids: William B. Eerdmans Publishing Company, Reprint, 1978).

Chapter 3
1. O. A. Piper, "Gospel," in *The Interpreter's Dictionary of the Bible,* 4 vols. (Nashville: Abingdon Press, 1962-76), 2:444.
2. Ibid., 443.
3. William Barclay, *New Testament Words* (Philadelphia: The Westminster Press, 1974), 104.
4. Ibid.
5. R. Abba, "Propitiation" in *The Interpreter's Dictionary of the Bible,* 4 vols. (Nashville: Abingdon Press, 1962-76), 3:920.
6. Ibid.,
7. Ibid., 3:921.
8. Adolf Deissmann, *Bible Studies.* (Edinburgh: T. & T. Clark, 1909), 125-135.
sl11
Chapter 4
1. Herwart Vorlander, "Corban" in *The New International Dictionary of New Testament Theology,* ed. by Colin Brown, 3 vols. (Grand Rapids: Zondervan Publishing House, 1976), 2:40.
2. Ibid., 42.
3. Charles C. Ryrie, *The Ryrie Study Bible* (Chicago: Moody Press,

dencion Viva, 1983), 12.

5. John MacArthur, *The Gospel According to Jesus* (Grand Rapids: Academic Books, 1988), 161.

6. The synonym *dechomai* also means "to receive" and is used several times to denote receiving the Word of God (See Acts 8:14; 17:11; 22:18; 1 Thess. 1:6; 2:13). *Apodechomai* is used in Acts 2:41. Once it is used of receiving Christ (Luke 9:48). In Luke 18:17 it refers to receiving the kingdom of God. There is no discernible difference between *lambano* and *dechomai* in meaning. In fact, in several passages they are interchanged (Matt. 13:20; Luke 8:13).

7. Otto Michel, "Faith" in *The New International Dictionary of New Testament Theology*, 3 vols. (Grand Rapids: Zondervan Publishing House, 1975-78), 1:595.

8. Other examples of *epistrepho* relating to conversion include Acts 15:19; 26:18; 2 Corinthians 3:16; 1 Peter 2:25. The conversion of Israel is mentioned in Matthew 13:15; Mark 4:12; Luke 1:16; and Acts 28:27.

9. B. F. Westcott, *The Gospel According to St. John* (London: James Clarke & Company, 1958), reprint.

10. Adolf Deissmann, *Light from the Ancient East*, Ibid., 121.

11. Everett F. Harrison and John R. Stott, "Must Christ Be Lord to Be Savior?" *Eternity* (September 1959): 16.

12. Charles C. Ryrie, *Balancing the Christian Life* (Chicago: Moody, 1969), 173-175.

13. Harrison and Stott, Ibid., 16.

14. Ibid., 15.

15. R. C. H. Lenski, *The Interpretation of St. Matthew's Gospel* (Minneapolis: Augsburg Publishing House, 1961, reprint), 627.

16. Ibid., 626.

17. Ibid., 628.

18. A list of scholars who have realized the implications of the perfect participle here is given in *Light from the Greek New Testament* by Boyce W. Blackwelder (Grand Rapids: Baker Book House, 1976), 78-80.

19. Julius R. Mantey in *Was Peter a Pope?* (Chicago: Moody Press, 1949, 51) points out that Jerome incorrectly translated this verse in the Latin Vulgate (ca. A.D. 400).

20. Lenski, Ibid.

21. Ibid.

Chapter 5
1. H. H. Esser, " Creation" in *The New International Dictionary of New Testament Theology*, Ibid., 1:378.
2. H. Seebass, "Righteousness" in *The New International Dictionary of New Testament Theology*, Ibid., 3:355. House, 1975-78), 3:355.
3. Ibid., 371.
4. W. A. Criswell, editor, *The Criswell Study Bible* (Nashville: Thomas Nelson, 1979), 1108.
5. Ibid.
6. P. E. Hughes, *Paul's Second Epistle to the Corinthians* (Grand Rapids: Wm. B. Eerdmans, l962), 434.
7. B. F. Westcott, *The Epistle to the Hebrews* (London: Macmillan and Company, 1920), 107.
8. Hughes, Ibid., 433.

Chapter 6
1. J. B. Lightfoot, *Saint Paul's Epistle to the Galatians* (London: Macmillan and Company, 1877), 204.
2. Ernest De Witt Burton, *The Epistle to the Galatians* in the *International Critical Commentary* (Edinburgh: T. & T. Clark, 1921), 276. 276.
3. Burton, Ibid., 277.
4. W. V. Martitz, *"huiothesia"* in *Theological Dictionary of the New Testament, edited by* Gerhard Kittel and Gerhard Friedrich. 10 vols. translated by Geoffrey W. Bromiley (Grand Rapids: William B. Eerdmans, 1972), 8:398.
5. William Barclay, *The Letter to the Romans* in *The Daily Study Bible* (Edinburgh: The Saint Andrew Press, 1955), 110-111.
6. F. F. Bruce, *The Epistle to the Hebrews* in the *New International Commentary on the New Testament* (Grand Rapids: William B. Eerdmans, 1964), 118-122.
7. Wuest, *Hebrews in the Greek New Testament in Wuest's Word Studies*, 3 vols. (Grand Rapids: William B. Eerdmans, 1973), 2:113*ff.*
8. Ernest D. Schmitz, "Knowledge" in *The New International Dictionary of New Testament Theology*, 3 vols. (Grand Rapids: Zondervan Publishing House, 1975-78), 2:392.
9. Ibid., 2:399.

Index of New Testament References

Bibliography

Barclay, William. *New Testament Words.* Philadelphia: The Westminster Press, 1964.

_____. Bauer, Walter. *A Greek-English Lexicon of the New Testament and Other Early Christian Literature.* Fourth ed. Translated and edited by William F. Arndt and F. Wilbur Gingrich. Chicago: University of Chicago Press, 1952.

Blackwelder, Boyce W. *Light from the Greek New Testament.* Grand Rapids: Baker Book House, 1976.

Brown, Colin, ed. *Dictionary of New Testament Theology,* 3 Vols. Grand Rapids: Zondervan Publishing House, 1976.

Bruce, F. F. "The Epistle to the Hebrews" in the *New International Commentary on the New Testament.* Grand Rapids: Wm. B. Eerdmans Publishing Company, 1964.

Burton, Ernest DeWitt. "The Epistle to the Galatians" in the *International Critical Commentary.* Edinburgh: T. & T. Clark, 1921.

Cocoris, G. Michael. *Lordship Salvation   Is It Biblical?* Dallas, Texas: Redencion Viva, 1983.

Deissman, Adolf. *Bible Studies.* Edinburgh: T. & T. Clark, 1909.

_____. *Light from the Ancient East.* New York: George H. Doran, 1927.

Hendrickson, William. *The Gospel of Matthew.* Grand Rapids: Baker Book House, 1973.

Hughes, P. E. *Paul's Second Epistle to the Corinthians.* Grand Rapids: William B. Eerdmans Publishing Company, 1962.

Kittel, Gerhard, and Friedrich, Gerhard. *Theological Dictionary of the New Testament,* 10 Vols. Grand Rapids: William B. Eerdmans Publishing Company, 1972.

Lenski, R. C. H. *The Interpretation of Saint Matthew's Gospel.* Minneapolis: Augsburg Publishing House, 1961 reprint.

Lightfoot, J. B. *Saint Paul's Epistle to the Galatians.* London: Macmillan and Company, *1887.*

MacArthur, John. *The Gospel According to Jesus.* Grand Rapids: Academic Books, 1988.

Milligan, George. *Selections from the Greek Papyri.* Freeport, N.Y.: Books for Libraries Press, Reprint of the 1910 edition, 1969.

Moulton, James Hope, and Milligan, George. *The Vocabulary of the Greek*

New Testament. Grand Rapids: William B. Eerdmans Publishing Company, Reprint of the 1930 edition, 1982.

Nicoll, W. Robertson, editor. *The Expositor's Greek Testament, 5 Vols. Grand Rapids: William B. Eerdmans Reprint, 1974.*

Robertson, A. T. *Word Pictures in the New Testament.* 6 Vols. Nashville: Broadman Press, 1931.

Ryrie, Charles C. *Balancing the Christian Life.* Chicago: Moody Press, 1969.

Thayer, Joseph Henry. *A Greek-English Lexicon of the New Testament.* Edinburgh: T. & T. Clark, Fourth ed., 1901.

Trench, Richard C. *Synonyms of the New Testament.* Grand Rapids: William B. Eerdmans Publishing Company, Reprint of the 1880 edition, 1975.

Vine, W. E. *Vine's Expository Dictionary of New Testament Words.* McLean, Virginia: MacDonald Publishing Company, 1939.

Westcott, B. F. *The Epistle to the Hebrews.* London: Macmillan and Company, 1920.

Wuest, Kenneth S. *Wuest's Word Studies.* Four Vols. Grand Rapids: William B. Eerdmans Publishing Company, Reprint, 1978.